EARTHFIRE

The MIT Press

Cambridge, Massachusetts

London, England

EARTHFIRE

The Eruption of Mount St. Helens

Charles Rosenfeld and Robert Cooke

This book was set in Univers by Graphic Composition, Inc., and printed and bound by Halliday Lithograph in the United States of America.

Library of Congress Cataloging in Publication Data

Rosenfeld, Charles.
 Earthfire: the eruption of Mount St. Helens.

 Bibliography: p.
 Includes index.
 1. Saint Helens, Mount (Wash.)—Eruption, 1980. I. Cooke, Robert, 1935–   . II. Title.
QE523.S23R67 1982 551.2'1'0979784 82–9969
ISBN 0–262–18106–1   AACR2

Contents

List of Technical Vignettes

Acknowledgments

We wish to thank the following faculty members of Oregon State University for contributing technical vignettes to the work: Alan N. Federman, School of Oceanography, Department of Geological Oceanography; Michael Fehler, School of Oceanography, Department of Geophysics; Albert E. Frank, Department of Atmospheric Sciences; and Robert S. Yeats, Department of Geology. We thank the Oregonian for giving permission to reprint the vignette by Robert S. Yeats, which appeared in the Oregonian on December 7, 1980.

All photographs are by Charles Rosenfeld unless otherwise cited.

EARTHFIRE

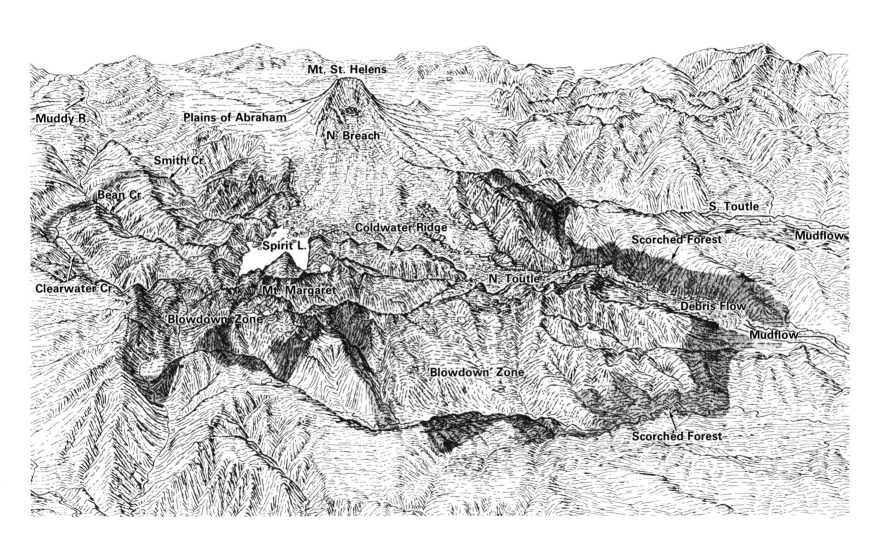

Locations of prominent features within the volcanic devastation zone around Mount St. Helens; view is toward the south. After Tau Rho Alpha, U.S. Geological Survey, 1980.

Mt. St. Helens

Muddy R.

Plains of Abraham

N. Breach

Smith Cr.

Bean Cr.

S. Toutle

Coldwater Ridge

Scorched Forest

Mudflows

Spirit L.

Clearwater Cr.

N. Toutle

Mt. Margaret

Debris Flow

Blowdown Zone

Mudflow

Blowdown Zone

Scorched Forest

1 | *Northwest Cataclysm*

Dawn broke bright and clear over the horizon that Sunday, back-lighting the beautiful silhouette of Mount St. Helens against a brightening eastern sky. It was quiet, quieter than it had been in the past 2 months, as the world began to wake and stir.

Campers, adding tinder, fanned coals to get breakfast going, rolled their sleeping bags in preparation for another day in the lush, green Pacific Northwest forest. It was May 18, 1980, first day of the new trout season, first good weather of spring.

They knew they were close, but not too close, they thought, to the steep, trembling cone of the big volcano. It seemed quiet enough, and safe enough, to get on with enjoying the outdoors. .

Above, an army surveillance plane skimmed low, making lazy passes close to the mountain's snow-clad summit. Readings were taken of changing heat flow patterns in the peak; then the plane circled, turned back, heading home toward Oregon.

Two hours later, high above, in a light plane looking down on the forest, down on the rivers and the mountain's high, bare slopes, geologists Keith and Dorothy Stoffel—overhead at the moment Mount St. Helens exploded—had the best ringside seat. Keith Stoffel's impressions:

Within a matter of seconds, perhaps 15 seconds, the whole north side of the summit crater began to move, instantaneously. As we were looking directly down on the summit crater, everything north of a line drawn east/west across the northern side began to move as one gigantic mass.

The nature of the movement was eerie, like nothing we had ever seen before. The entire mass began to ripple and churn up, without moving laterally. Then the entire north side of the mountain began sliding to the north along a deep-seated slide plane.

I was amazed and excited with the realization that we were watching this landslide of unbelievable proportions slide down the north side of the mountain toward Spirit Lake.

On the ground, at the Coldwater II observation post just 8 kilometers north of the summit, geologist David A. Johnston quickly manned his radio: "Vancouver! Vancouver! This is it. . . ."

He was never heard from again. Johnston, 30, a geologist-volcanologist employed by the US Geological Survey, was directly in the path of the directed blast of hot debris that burst from the side of the volcano. Rescue crews, flown in by helicopter, later found no trace of Johnston or his observation post. His campsite was found littered with large boulders, ash, and broken tree trunks, but there was no sign of life.

Johnston had camped at the observation post hoping to use binoculars to examine a peculiar bulge that was building up below the rim of the crater. By then the awakening volcano had been rumbling and steaming for 8 weeks.

Along with Johnston, another 18 persons were soon known to have died, some 70 others were listed as missing or presumed dead, and another 130 lucky souls had been airlifted to safety by rescue teams in helicopters. Among the missing was Harry Truman, 84, who along with his 16 cats lived in a lodge near Spirit Lake, also about 5 miles (8 kilometers) north of the mountain. Weeks earlier, Truman had refused to leave the area, stating to a television crew, "No one knows more about this mountain than Harry, and it don't dare blow up on him."

After the blast, Harry's homestead was buried deep beneath a steaming miasma of hot mud, water, and broken forest debris.

The eruption, indeed, had totally destroyed 123 buildings and everything in the Toutle Valley, including bridges, roads, and any other sign of human habitation.

To say this tremendous explosion was a surprise would be an understatement. Using the Oregon National Guard's powerful Mohawk aircraft, Capt. Charles Rosenfeld had flown reconaissance missions earlier in the weekend, and the thermal infrared measurements did show changing heat patterns, but nothing exceptional. On Friday evening, May 16, for example, signs of increased thermal activity were detected outside the summit crater, in the area of the false summit and The Boot, and extending on down to the Goat Rocks area. At that time, the Goat Rocks dome was thermally cool.

On Saturday, May 17, on another run, the same heating pattern was seen, especially down in the bulge area, where there were a few intermittent hot spots.

And, finally, on Sunday, May 18, at 5:52 A.M. (Pacific Daylight Time), the last thermal run was made before the big explosion. Essentially the same hot spots were seen and, contrary to what was written in some articles, there was no obvious cause for alarm in the results from this last thermal run before the explosion.

There was obviously some increased heating outside the crater and in the bulge area, but there was nothing that would have been predictive of an explosive eruption of the magnitude that occurred within the next 2 hours.

Until that fateful morning—May 18, 1980—quiet, serene Mount St. Helens had been known as the Mount Fuji of the Northwest. The young volcanic peak, one of 14 large volcanoes in the Cascade system, was renowned for its beautiful symmetry, especially when seen reflected in the still waters of Spirit Lake. But in the time between March 20 and the May 18 cataclysm, this awesomely beautiful mountain had been warning, not so subtly, that something big was coming. And what the Stoffels saw while flying overhead was the first instant of what quickly became the biggest, most impressive, and deadly volcanic eruption seen by modern Americans in their own country. The sequence of events during that massive eruption, pieced together later, went something like this:

First, at 8:32 A.M. (Pacific Daylight Time), an earthquake of Richter magnitude 4.9 seemed to shake loose an unstable area on the north side of the peak, the area known as Goat Rocks, triggering the massive landslide that Stoffel saw from above. This landslide, which occurred on the side of the mountain that had been bulging outward at the incredible rate of 5 feet (1.5 meters) per day since mid-April, probably reduced pressure on the superheated groundwater close to the magma, allowing the water to flash into steam, loosing a high-velocity flow of steam and ash to go racing down across the Toutle River Valley.

As this steam explosion intensified, overlying rocks were quickly broken up and began surging laterally to form a rapidly moving debris flow. Moving as a cascade of superheated material, it quickly swept down the mountain's flanks, filling up much of the Spirit Lake Basin.

As the summit graben collapsed, two large vertical blast columns erupted, which may have triggered the explosive release of dissolved magmatic gases. This, in turn, pushed up a large vertical ash-laden plume from the breached crater, progressively removing the south wall of the crater and bringing the summit elevation down from 9,525 feet (2,903 meters) to 8,170 feet (2,490 meters), decapitating the mountain by more than 1,300 feet (400 meters).

Early observers estimated the blast released energy equivalent to a nuclear bomb 500 times larger than the one dropped on Hiroshima, Japan, toward the end of World War II. Some estimated the mountain spewed out 1.5 cubic miles (50 million cubic meters) of debris, sending most of it roaring miles down the river valleys, pouring the rest of it into the atmosphere to be carried eastward with the wind across most of the state of Washington, into Idaho, Montana, and beyond.

Given this scenario, then, the lateral blast—which tossed ash, soil, rocks and blocks of ice as far as 12 miles (20 kilometers) to the north and east—probably involved a combination of steam and explosive gas releases that mixed with pulverized rock materials from the mountain's north flank. It formed into a dense, high-speed cloud, heated to about 600°F (300°C), that stormed down the mountain, topping ridges, filling valleys, and wiping out vegetation for miles around.

In some cases, the devastation was extreme, unbelievably complete. Near the breached northern flank of the mountain, almost every exposed slope within a 6-mile (10-kilometer) radius was completely denuded of all vegetation and covered by up to 7 feet (2 meters) of ash and debris.

Beyond this, at about 9 miles (15 kilometers) radius, large trees were snapped off at the ground and their felled trunks were completely stripped of branches. Remaining stumps were partially buried by the ashfall. Trees on the protected leeward sides of hills were left standing, but their foliage was badly singed. And, in a zone that extended from 335 to 1,005 feet (100 to 300 meters) beyond this, trees' needles and branches were either stripped off or the needles were at least singed to an orange color.

During that big explosion, the more solid blocks of rock from the volcano's north flank were heaved across the Toutle Valley and the Spirit Lake Basin. Indeed, huge blocks from the Goat Rocks dome—some of them 67 feet (20 meters) in diameter—were later found resting 5 miles (8 kilometers) to the north, on the northwest arm of Spirit Lake, where they were apparently deposited by the force of the blast or by the flow of debris. It was estimated, too, that the water in Spirit Lake was sloshed nearly 1,000 feet (300 meters) up the south side of nearby Mount Margaret.

Before word of the explosive eruption arrived, Captain Rosenfeld, based at Salem, Oregon, had been planning on flying the second mission to the mountain that day after the first heat readings were taken early in the morning. But the news of Mount St. Helens's sudden, explosive eruption sent Rosenfeld and Chief Warrant Officer John Sedey rushing for their waiting OV-1 Mohawk aircraft. They were quickly airborne, and Rosenfeld recalled,

My own first glimpse of the mountain after the explosion came at 9:10 A.M., as John and I flew around to the west side for our initial passes. Our first objective was search and rescue, and we were trying to verify the condition of the two observation posts on Coldwater Ridge.

The US Geological Survey's observation post, manned by David Johnston, had consisted of a travel trailer and a four-wheel-drive vehicle. We found nothing but a gray, utterly devastated landscape, reminiscent of the moon's bare surface.

At first, too, we couldn't tell whether we were seeing pyroclastic flows descending down the north slope of the volcano, or whether a breach had indeed occurred, blowing out the north wall toward Spirit Lake.

As we came up over Coldwater Ridge, we began to notice that the eruption plume was heading up, like a mushroom cloud, and beginning to unfurl overhead. We made a pass into the vicinity of Spirit Lake, then did a quick turnaround and proceeded down the Toutle River Valley once again. We were unable to see the ground, and we were becoming somewhat disturbed that we were being overtopped by the ash plume.

As we came back around to the west side, the big mushroom cloud was unfurling over our heads, and we watched as low stratus clouds were entrained, or literally sucked into the plume. We passed within 200 or 300 meters of the plume—which seemed like a vertical wall of gray-brown debris—several times. As we passed by this eruptive plume, immediately off our wingtips we could see the column eddying and swirling as it rose to altitudes of more than 50,000 or 60,000 feet. This main eruptive plume, carrying tons and tons of ash, travelled nearly 4,000 miles before the day was over.

By noon, however, the eruption plume had become less violently convulsive, but it was accompanied by large pyroclastic debris flows boiling down the northwest flank of the mountain, crashing into the Toutle River Valley below, causing quite a large cloud of steam to rise out of the valley. We presumed what was left of the Toutle River was being flashed into steam by those hot pyroclastic flows.

Later in the day, we launched another Oregon National Guard OV-1 Mohawk aircraft, this one equipped with side-looking airborne radar, since our thermal sensors were unable to see anything through the dense cover of ash and dust at ground level. That afternoon we were able to gain the first clear view of Mount St. Helens by transmitting the radar signals down through the ash plume itself. We were able to see very clearly the outline of the crater and very firmly establish that the north flank of the mountain had been breached wide open.

We were unable to detect Spirit Lake, however, because of the tremendous amount of flotsam—trees, debris, and pumice—floating on the surface. These reflected the radar return so it looked as if there was no longer a Spirit Lake.

Our moving-target channel on the radar, which enables us to distinguish moving objects from fixed objects, also showed us the movements of the mud flows and debris flows.

A little later in the afternoon, too, we were able to get some clear views of the ground near the mountain. The first thing that came into view was the huge debris flow that had come out of the north breach and had continued westward down the North Toutle River Valley. This flow was up to 4 or 5 kilometers in width, and we measured it going westward for about 28 kilometers.

In addition we were able to get a few views to the north and west of the tremendous blowdown damage in the forests. The farthest west we were able to see the blowdown was 23 kilometers. It appeared that the blast had literally skipped over various ridges, leaving standing the trees on the leeward side, but completely removing the trees on the exposed side. North of the mountain the destruction was incredible. The entire forest had been stripped away, including even the roots of the trees and in places as much as 3 feet of soil. Dust and steam were rising everywhere as the steam explosions continued.

There were many bizarre forms in the Toutle River Valley, including what appeared to be explosion vents, from what we now recognize were steam explosions. In other words, the hot pyro-

clastic debris was coming into contact with water seeping out of the Spirit Lake area. This produced steam explosions, one of which actually opened up a crater almost a half-mile long in the North Toutle River Valley.

The next day, on May 19, we began to get our first detailed views of the ground around Mount St. Helens. The eruption had finally tapered off by about 3:30 A.M. that morning.

A real feel for the devastation caused by the lateral blast on the 18th didn't really hit home with us until we took that first flight up on the 19th. The small bits and pieces of the blowdown area that we had seen earlier hadn't been nearly as impressive as this first full view of the 400-square-kilometer area of blowdown.

On the other side of the mountain one could see incredible mudflows that had come down Pine Creek, Smith Creek, and the Muddy River. These mudflows engulfed entire forests, sometimes covering as much as 3,200 acres (1,300 hectares) with a single lobe of mud. Between the mudflows, the forests were often on fire, apparently ignited by lightning or the hot ash debris.

At Swift Reservoir, these mudflows joined so as to create a large delta that extended over half a mile (1 kilometer) into the reservoir. There, millions of board feet of logs came to rest, having been literally harvested in one fell swoop before being swept into the reservoir by the cascade of mud.

By then the helicopter rescue effort was just getting under way, and the Oregon National Guard team spent most of the day helping locate helicopters that were getting lost in the low-level dust and ash. The Mohawk was flown up and down the valleys trying to spot victims, looking for survivors moving along the roads. Rosenfeld continued:

During the night, with radar, we had picked up moving targets, vehicles, that were apparently trying to find their way out of the area, but they were cut off by missing bridges, or by areas where the road was buried by mudflows.

Mostly, however, we just came across vehicles within the blowdown area, and no signs of life were visible. We spotted several such locations, marked them, and reported them to the Washington State Emergency Services, but to our knowledge no survivors were found in any of the vehicles we spotted.

Left:
During early stages of the eruption this dark gray plume developed as phreatic explosions and quickly hollowed out the core of the mountain, forming the large open-sided crater.

Right:
The eruptive plume, shown boiling up from the breached north flank of the mountain.

The dark eruption plume ascending from the roaring mountain begins rising to high altitude, unfurling to form the large mushroom head.

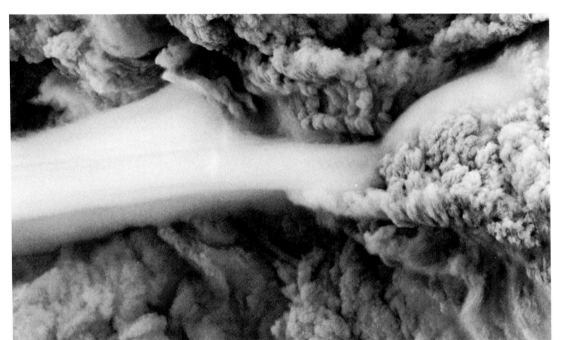

Left:
View taken during a pass close to the eruption plume, showing clouds being entrained into the rapidly rising eruption plume.

Below:
The bottom of the mushroom cloud expands, as seen from below, at about 10 kilometers altitude. At the lower left can be seen the vertical plume climbing up from the breached crater of Mount St. Helens.

Three hot pyroclastic flows can be seen descending the mountain's northwest flank shortly after noon on the day of the large eruption. At the same time, at left, an 8,300-foot- (2,500-meter-) high steam plume can be seen coming from the North Toutle River valley. The steam erupts from explosions in the hot ash debris that flooded the valley.

Left:
View taken from an altitude of 13,300 feet (4,000 meters), showing the North Toutle River valley debris flow at about 2 P.M. on the day of the massive blast. In the center, a search plane can be seen flying only about 1,700 feet (500 meters) above the debris flow.

Below:
View west along the North Toutle River valley, showing where the lateral blast moved debris—from left to right—to overtop Coldwater Ridge. Most of the material had become fluidized, allowing it to flow toward the west down the valley floor.

View to the east, looking across the North Toutle River valley debris flow toward Mount St. Helens.

In all, the eruption blew down about 150 square miles (400 square kilometers) of prime timber containing more than 3.2 billion board feet of lumber worth about $200 million. It also caused damage estimated at $222 million to wheat, alfalfa, corn, and other crops across a large portion of the Pacific Northwest.

On the ground during the blast, too, a group of fishermen, trapped on the Green River, 16 miles (26 kilometers) northeast of the peak, found themselves near the periphery of the devastated area. They were badly burned, and survived only by jumping into the river when they first became aware of the explosion. They suffered burns, however, when they came up for air, and when they left the protection of the water. The heat, they said, came in waves, over a period lasting perhaps 10 or 15 minutes.

At Ryan Lake, 13 miles (21 kilometers) north-northeast of Mount St. Helens, rescue teams found that all the plastic parts on an overturned truck had been melted by the heat.

But there was some luck involved, too. If the volcanic blast from Mount St. Helens had come just one day later, on a Monday, a 200-man crew of lumbermen employed by the Weyerhauser Company would have been working in the area, felling, limbing, and transporting trees. No one knows how many might have been killed or injured by the blast.

In later analyses of the sequence of events, research teams have been able to decipher in better detail what probably happened on May 18th. It appears now that the initial landslide probably moved en masse to the bottom of the Toutle Valley, where it broke up and was intermixed with the ash and pulverized rock being carried by the directed blast.

The momentum of this flow shoved debris over the crest of Coldwater Ridge, which acted as a barrier standing 1,200 feet (350 meters) above the floor of the Toutle Valley. In most of these areas, the forest was quickly removed and soils were indeed scoured to a depth of more than 3 feet (1 meter).

Also, a huge debris fan spread north from the breached crater wall, depositing itself in Spirit Lake. This fan displaced the south shore of the lake by nearly 1,100 yards (1 kilometer), causing the level of the lake to rise by 120 feet (40 meters). To the west, this spreading fan of debris slammed against Coldwater Ridge and was then deflected westward down the once beautiful Toutle River Valley.

Since it was fluidized by the presence of groundwater and melting ice, the surge of rock debris and ash flowed rapidly for about 17 miles (28 kilometers) along the valley floor. It eventually came to rest against a small hill dividing the river's channel. As a result of this flow, parts of the valley floor were filled to a depth of about 200 feet (60 meters), with trimlines along the upper end of the river valley visible almost 400 feet (120 meters) above the former position of the valley floor.

After coming to rest in the hot debris, large blocks of glacial ice from the mountain's flanks melted, forming kettle holes in the surface or collapse pits when ice melted below the surface. Occasionally the meltwater or the groundwater contacted pockets of still hot ash, causing minor steam explosions that blasted small craters in the gray debris blanket.

Fortunately, however, a 200-foot- (70-meter-) high wall of ash and mud from the volcano, which had been deposited at the outlet of Spirit Lake, began leaking just enough to allow the backed-up water to escape, ending immediate fears that it would suddenly give way and loose another flood down the tortured Toutle Valley toward Castle Rock, Kelso, and Longview, where some 50,000 people live.

Earlier, however, surges of mud-laden floodwaters had gone sweeping down the channel of the Toutle River, washing out the previous channel, cutting away the banks and digging big holes in the riverbank. As the flood crest swept by Camp Baker, most of the logs stored there were picked up and carried downstream to jam against bridges, knocking them down. The flow of logs and wooden debris finally created a huge, 20-mile- (32-kilometer-) long log jam along the Columbia River.

Similar flooding occurred on the south fork of the Toutle River as rapid deglaciation took place on the volcano's west flank.

These floods then combined and pushed into the Cowlitz River near Castle Rock, then flowed rapidly south, entering the wide Columbia River near Longview, Washington. There, within 24

View of the south shore of Spirit Lake, where it was suddenly dammed by a pockmarked debris flow.

Below:
Even 40 kilometers west of Mount St. Helens, the flow of mud and debris clogs the channel of the Toutle River.

Right:
A nuée ardente, or hot pyroclastic debris flow, is seen descending the western flank of Mount St. Helens. The leading edge of this avalanche can be seen surging several meters ahead of the main cloud of broiling-hot steam and ash.

hours, huge deposits of sediment built up to form a delta, quickly reducing the depth of the Columbia River from 40 feet (12 meters) to less than 10 feet (4 meters), blocking most navigation and essentially isolating the busy harbor at Portland, Oregon. The loss of shipping business alone, not counting the cost of dredging the channel to its normal depth, was expected to cost ports on the Columbia some $5 million per day.

On the eastern side of the mountain, pyroclastic flows went pouring down the steep flanks, also creating mudflows. The rapid, heavy accumulations of hot ash melted the snowfields on Mount St. Helens's northeast flank, loosing a mud-rich flow that spread widely over the Abraham Plains. This flow then continued on to drain into the Muddy River.

Rapid deglaciation of the upper Shoestring Glacier's cirque let loose another of those large mudflows. This then joined with the surge in the Muddy River and poured into the Swift Reservoir, raising the level of that lake by over half a meter.

After the blast it became evident that the May 18 eruption of Mount St. Helens can be accurately described as a true Peléan eruption. That term, in general, refers to very violent eruptions, of an explosive nature, in which large amounts of pumice are erupted quickly because of the large amount of volatile gases dissolved in the magma. In addition, the hot, incandescent clouds of steam and ash known as *nuées ardentes* that flash down the slopes of volcanoes are typical of these so-called Peléan eruptions.

In the air, boiling into the sky to an altitude of 65,000–80,000 feet (20,000–25,000 meters), the volcano's vertical plume of gas, ash, steam, and dust trailed off to the northeast. Inside that tall plume could be seen strong convective upwelling currents, while stratus clouds were entrained or "drawn in" at several levels within the vertical column. At the same time, violent flashes of lightning were seen throughout the height of the column, and as the mushroom cap formed, it began expanding outward at an altitude of about 50,000 feet (15,000 meters).

Observers flying close to that plume were able to see three very different altitudes of ash activity that lasted through the morning of May 18. At 80,000 feet (25,000 meters), a thin, stratoform layer formed and began to spread out. Below that, at about 30,000 feet (10,000 meters), a dense, nearly horizontal, serpentine plume, dripping large lobes of ash, was formed. And below 16,000 feet (5,000 meters), what appeared to be a layer of diffuse ash—perhaps suspended pulverized rock from the lateral blast—took shape.

From data gathered by a University of Washington atmospheric sampling plane, it was found that the median particle size in the dense ash plume—about 7 miles (12 kilometers) downwind from the blasted-open crater—was about 1 micrometer. This seems consistent with the particle sizes recorded in the maximum ashfall areas in eastern Washington State. Thus it is probable that these low-level ash clouds provided most of the local downwind ashfall, while the tall main plume held most of its ash until reaching eastern Washington State, where significant ashfall began.

Photos returned from satellites, too, indicate that the leading edge of the Mount St. Helens volcanic plume crossed the Idaho border by about 11 A.M., then entered Montana by about 3 P.M. the same day, May 18.

As winds spread this burden of ash, it fell in thick, fluffy layers that looked rather like dirty snow. Some 90 miles (140 kilometers) east of the volcano, in Yakima, the city's 50,000 residents were greeted with midnight at noon.

Farther east—in Idaho's panhandle and into western Montana—the streets and walks were largely abandoned. People moved about carefully, masked like bandits, and in some locations driving was almost impossible because of volcanic dust clogging air filters and other equipment. Factories, stores, schools, and offices were closed. Many highways were shut down, and airports were closed because of near-zero visibility. Thousands of travelers were stranded, frightened, in unfamiliar quarters. Mail was halted, and electric power was limited while workmen tried to clean the dust from generating equipment.

But, given time and effort, traffic did resume, and the long job of cleaning up began. It was an experience few who live in the Pacific Northwest will soon forget. And, close to the mountain, it was hard to predict how long recovery would take.

Thus was a huge area of beautiful wilderness destroyed almost instantly, cataclysmically. And thus was a huge, richly endowed agricultural area blanketed with an unwelcome new ingredient. Also, close to the mountain, where herds of deer and elk once thrived, where bobcats and cougers hunted in quiet woods, was nothing but devastation. The area's rich chinook salmon and steelhead trout fisheries were virtually wiped out—for years at least. The Toutle River, and its source, Spirit Lake, once rich in fish, had been an angler's paradise. At least a million fingerling salmon were killed in the hatchery at Toutle alone, and fisheries experts reported that some tagged fish were apparently going up the wrong rivers after the eruption. Their own spawning grounds—and the rivers, streams, and creeks leading to them—were completely choked with mud.

2 | *The Awakening*

Excitement, curiosity, even the hint of danger were powerful forces that began attracting people to the edge of the danger zone, to the boundaries of the "red zone" set up around Mount St. Helens soon after the volcano reawakened on March 20, 1980, abruptly ending a 123-year period of dormancy.

Indeed, the repeated warnings, the roadblocks, and the urgent pleas from government authorities probably catalyzed the spectators' enthusiasm. News of a nearby erupting volcano was enough to spur people into their campers, pickups, and sedans in hopes of seeing Mount St. Helens in action. They yearned for snapshots, even close-ups, of the tall mountain spitting ash and steam from its summit crater. After all, it isn't every day one sees Nature's forces unleashed on such grand scale.

Unfortunately, on May 18 they got much more than anyone expected, when in one cataclysmic blast a whole side of the mountain was blown away and the sky was filled with hot, choking ash, gas, and dust. Even weeks later, when authorities had sorted out most of the casualties, 62 men, women, and children were known or presumed to be dead, and a score or more were still listed as missing.

As should be recalled, however, this huge volcanic blast from Mount St. Helens did not come without warning. This, the first eruption of the mountain in a century and a quarter, had been several months in coming, first heralded at 3:47 P.M., Pacific Standard Time, on March 20, 1980, by a burst of underground tremors. The warning came in the form of earthquakes, the strongest of which registered at Richter magnitude 4. Soon the underground rumbling grew into a swarm of earthquakes of increasing intensity, continuing through the afternoon of March 25.

Seismologists noted that this March 20 sequence of tremors was unlike any other ever recorded in the Pacific Northwest, and probably in all of the contiguous United States. So it seemed something new was happening, something ominous beneath the tall cone of Mount St. Helens.

This sudden awakening of activity promptly caught the attention of the Pacific Northwest's earth scientists, who moved into action swiftly. There was little information to go on, however, even after instrumented planes flew over the 9,500-foot (2,950-meter) mountain on March 24 and found no evidence of new volcanic activity on the peak. But airborne observers did see evidence of recent avalanches, which had apparently been triggered by the earthquake activity. Then, as seismic activity continued, only a day later airborne observers spotted some new fractures in the glaciers high on the mountain, plus some large new rockfalls.

As the tremors continued, a great deal of effort went into locating the hypocenters for these earthquakes under the mountain. Early on, the western Washington seismic network located the earthquakes as occurring directly beneath the volcano's northwest flank. It was still difficult to determine the depths of these tremors, but there was no doubt that they were quite shallow.

As more instruments were added, however, the data improved. It was found that most activity was located up to 1 mile (1.6 kilometers) north of the mountain's summit. It was also found that most earthquakes were occurring at a depth of 2 miles (3.2 kilometers), a few were happening as deep as 6 miles (10 kilometers), and there was also a grouping of earthquake foci only 3,000 feet (1 kilometer) deep.

The first eruption from the peak came 2 days later, on Thursday, March 27, during early afternoon hours. Thick cloud cover had hidden the peak from view for at least 2 days, but several people reported hearing a loud concussion sound shortly after noon that day. Observers in aircraft also reported seeing a thick column of black smoke, probably ash, pushing up through the cloud cover. Within several hours this plume of ash reached a height of 6,500 feet (2,000 meters) above the cone.

Later that afternoon, too, the weather began to clear, allowing a number of good observations to be made from aircraft. Observers found that several conspicuous changes had occurred on Mount St. Helens, including the formation of a new crater some 220 feet (70 meters) in diameter in a northern area of the existing summit crater. The older crater, about 1,300 feet (400 meters) in diameter, was still ice filled, with the Shoestring Glacier penetrating its wall on the southeast.

This new activity brought personnel from the US Geological Survey's Volcanic Hazards and Tephra Hazards projects into the action. Donal R. Mullineaux arrived in Vancouver, Washington,

shortly after the initial earthquakes heralded the possible beginning of an eruption, to advise the US Forest Service on the possible hazards. After the first eruption, on March 27, a volcanic-hazards map was prepared through use of the Forest Service's existing maps of the Gifford Pinchot National Forest and adjacent regions. The map was used to outline the expected hazards from tephra, pyroclastic flows, and mudflows. Three possible levels of hazard were established according to whether volcanic activity became high, intermediate or low. Eventually, this map was used by the Forest Service and local agencies to define the areas near the volcano where public access would be limited. Such maps were also used for briefing groups of officials and residents of the area near the mountain.

Soon, however, the landslide dangers associated with the rapidly building bulge on the mountain's north flank became obvious, and a new map was prepared to show the public what areas might be affected.

Also, in anticipation of possible mudflows from the volcano, which might loose a massive flow into the Swift Reservoir, officials of the Pacific Power and Light Company began lowering the water level in the reservoir by late March. The company, which operates the hydroelectric plant at Swift Dam, kept the reservoir's level sufficiently low so that the lake could accept as much as 100 acre feet or 165 million cubic yards (125 million cubic meters) of mixed mud and water.

What could also be seen from above—after this first episode of volcanic activity—was a new fracture system trending eastward across the peak. It was already 1,700 feet (500 meters) long extending from a point on the mountain's west flank across the old crater and then down the higher part of the eastern flank. A second fracture system, less continuous than the first, paralleled the bigger fracture, running just to the north of the crater's rim. It ran adjacent to a large uplifted block on the northern flank of the volcano.

These features, then, were apparently formed in that first blast of volcanic activity, probably in association with the seismic activity that began shaking the snow-capped peak.

While not all reports from observers were wholly reliable, there were reports of some people seeing the larger fracture move—

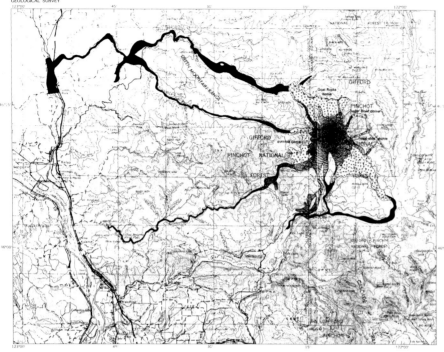

Predicted effects from eruption of Mount St. Helens, 1978. (Drawing courtesy of Crandell and Mollineaux, 1978)

opening and closing—and the mountain's northern flank rising during the first few hours after this first release of ash and gas.

A day later, Friday, March 28, a second rather explosive eruption was watched by airborne observers. It continued for only 2 hours, but it was sufficiently violent to produce a good portion of all the material released during the first sequence of eruptions. The ash from that Friday event came to the ground to the east of the volcano, spreading over a zone that was many miles long.

Further eruptions—some of them coming in staccato bursts only a few minutes long, others lasting as long as an hour—numbered up to a dozen or more that same day, March 28. These eruptions threw up a column of steam, gas, and ash to an altitude of 10,000 feet (3,000 meters) above the summit, but the heavier ejecta seldom rose more than 1,500 feet (500 meters) above the peak.

Finally, on March 29, observers got their first really clear views of the mountain. They were treated to a view of a second new crater that had opened up just to the west of the first one. It was already larger than the first crater, and was separated from it by a thin bridge, or septum, that was only about 35 feet (10 meters) wide. And that night, the first observations of a pale blue flame in association with the craters were made. The flame was seen at different times in each crater during the dark of night.

The eerie blue flame covered a zone estimated at from 10 to 20 feet (3 to 5 meters) in diameter in the smaller crater, and an area perhaps 50 feet (15 meters) in diameter in the larger crater, and once it flashed along a fracture that extended up the crater's western wall. Where the flame occurred seemed to vary, apparently in response to eruptive activity. Sometimes, indeed, within just a few minutes of the beginning of an eruption, the blue flame increased its diameter several times over. Once, too, the flame was seen to move from the east crater to the west crater, and twice it was seen at the same time in both craters.

Observations of the flame are considered important because it signaled the presence of flammable gases, indicating enough gas was there to ignite occasionally. Ignition could have been triggered either by lightning or other electric discharges or simply by high temperature.

Phreatic—or steam-blast—eruptions came from the western crater on April 2 and gradually destroyed the narrow wall separating the pair of craters.

No one was able to determine the composition of the gas that burned with a blue flame, but observers said they suspected the most important gas was hydrogen sulfide. Indeed, hydrogen sulfide was the only flammable gas detected when the eruptive plumes were sampled, and it requires relatively low temperatures for ignition.

Airborne observers were also able to see a number of ground-hugging ashflows that went sweeping down the sides of the mountain. These flows were first identified—mistakenly, as it turned out—as flows of hot ejecta from the craters, but it was soon discovered instead that they were wind driven. Often, too, during the downward sweep of these ashflows one could see spectacular bursts of horizontal or slope-parallel lightning discharging in the ash clouds.

New bursts of seismic activity, strange harmonic tremors this time, began on April 1, with some of these tremors lasting as long as 5 minutes. Even stronger bursts of seismic activity were recorded the following day, and some were detected with seismic instruments located as much as 60 miles (100 kilometers) away. Such tremors—apparently indicative of magma moving underground—continued sporadically over the next few days, until at least April 12. At the time, however, no obvious changes in the eruptions were correlated with the harmonic tremors. Through the rest of April, both the strength and frequency of these tremors declined, and volcanic activity atop the peak also seemed to taper off.

As both types of activity declined, however, the narrow septum that separated the two craters disappeared altogether, creating a single crater that kept enlarging until it was 1,700 feet (500 meters) long from east to west and 1,000 feet (300 meters) wide in the other direction. Also during the period, as the crater was enlarging, it continued to be the only place where steam and ash were being vented. And as the month wore on, the large crater began to deepen, eventually reaching a depth of about 700 feet (250 meters).

Field crews by then were doing tilt measurements on the volcano's flanks. A station located in the Timberline parking lot, for example, was occupied on seven occasions before April 30, and it measured a significant tilt (50 microradians) down to the north-east, away from the volcano. After frustrating efforts to measure the Timberline dry-tilt station, a 130-foot (40-meter) line was measured, and significant changes were seen occurring in only a matter of minutes. Over several days, then, several sessions of a few hours each were run, with readings being taken about every minute. In these measurements, tilts were observed in both inflationary and deflationary senses, with changes of 50 microradians occurring in less than an hour. In general, too, tilt vectors were either toward or away from the swelling Goat Rocks area, not the volcano's summit.

In an informal US Geological Survey communication concerning experiences on the mountain, D. A. Swanson noted, "While leveling during a major explosion on April 10, we noticed that the bulls-eye bubble, used for crude levelling of the instrument, was moving. We watched the bubble in awe for several minutes, then set up the monitor and began to record smaller, but no less dramatic, tilts."

In the meantime, the first good photometric measurements of the bulge—which had been noticed on Mount St. Helens's north flank—were reported. These data, for the first time, revealed the truly startling size and rate of expansion of the bulge. It had, indeed, been growing noticeably larger and more conspicuous since the first eruption. The highest point on the bulge, located north of the old crater rim, was almost 320 feet (100 meters) higher than any corresponding point on the north flank, while the Goat Rocks area had been moved to the northwest by more than 290 feet (90 meters). Some estimates held that the north flank was swelling, expanding outward, at a rate of as much as 15 feet (5 meters) per day.

As of April 22, however, eruptive activity essentially ceased, even though the earthquakes continued at a high, but declining, rate. The number of earthquakes of Richter magnitude 3 or above averaged close to 30 per day, and there were as many as 15 per day of Richter magnitude 4 or greater.

During this relatively quiescent period, fumeroles were seen to be venting continuously inside the crater. The largest of these was venting from the south wall of the crater, just above the

View from the north showing the crater on April 30, just before we used a helicopter to descend into the crater to measure the temperature of the heated ground. The size of the crater is shown by the helicopter parked on the ground at lower right.

Close-up view of the fumarole inside the crater at the base of the south wall. The temperature of the dark area surrounding the vent was 75°F (24°C), while the temperature of the gas and steam coming from the fumarole was 215°F (102°C). The steam plume from the fumarole is being blown downward by the helicopter's rotor wash.

crater floor. At least one attempt was made to sample the gases issuing from fumaroles, but this effort was abandoned because ice, avalanching down from the crater wall above the vents, made close approach impossible. Nonetheless, it was possible to sample the water from a small pond that had formed on the floor of the eastern part of the crater.

Studies of the ejecta being thrown from the crater showed that no new pyrogenic material was in the ash in March and April. Observers said the material associated with the steam eruptions was "rock flour", apparently produced by the grinding of rocks being tossed and jostled inside the vents. The ash that was released consisted mostly of poorly sorted crystals, crystal fragments, and grains. Pictures produced in the scanning electron microscope showed some rounding of the particles, indicating they may have been abraded and worn while in the vents.

During the early phases of the eruption—in March and April—ash and dust from the volcano were distributed in all directions within a radius of 31 miles (50 kilometers) and to at least 60 miles (100 kilometers) to the south and southeast. Ash was reported in the Tacoma area, some 60 miles (100 kilometers) to the north of the volcano, and unconfirmed reports had ash being detected 150 miles (250 kilometers) away, to the southeast, in Bend, Oregon.

Measurements of the gases released by Mount St. Helens were made after samples were gathered by aircraft flying through the volcanic plume. This was done by the University of Washington Cloud Physics Research Group on March 28, and they found that sulfur dioxide made up about 95 percent of the sulfurous gases in the samples. This was important because it indicated that a high-temperature source was releasing the gases to the surface during the steam eruptions.

Given the violence and massive size of Mount St. Helens's eruption, then, it seems likely that these events are just the first rounds in a long episode of activity. And although the magnitude and the violence of the explosive eruption of May 18 were certainly beyond anyone's expectations, the earth scientists who were assessing the eruptive hazards of the Mount St. Helens area should be gratified that their work was so effective.

Indeed, the precautions and safeguards provided by scientific workers and government agencies can be credited with substantially reducing the loss of life in the explosive eruption of Mount St. Helens, an event that can be reasonably compared to the blast of a 10-megaton nuclear bomb. (Dr. Susan W. Kieffer reporting in volume 291 of the journal Nature says that "from the measured mass ejected and the assumed initial temperature of 600°K (620°F) the total thermal energy released on cooling to ambient temperature was 10^{24} erg or 24 megatons, of which 7 megatons were released during the propagation of the blast through the devastated area, and 17 megatons during penecontemporaneous condensation of the steam and cooling of entrained solids.") In addition, the observations made—and the experience gained— should help the community of earth scientists learn to predict such eruptions with better accuracy in the future. At the same time, it may also help complex, modern societies deal more effectively with major disasters in the future.

3 | A History of Ice, Mud, and Fire

The feeling of peace, serenity, and quiet that draws people to the wooded mountains and cool streams of the Pacific Northwest are actually a facade, a thin disguise masking one of the most violently active geological regions in the United States. Despite the evidence of the senses, despite the singing of the birds, the wind whistling through fir trees, and quiet walks in the woods, the beautiful topography of western Washington and Oregon is subject to incredibly violent activity, especially volcanic activity. The Pacific Northwest, indeed, is a region of geological change, and the changes often come in tumultuous fits and starts that lay waste to vast tracts of virgin forest, thousands of acres of valuable croplands, and miles of waterways.

Given this history, then, it was with some confidence, back in 1975, that geologists Donal R. Mullineaux and Dwight R. Crandell were able to warn—bluntly, clearly—that Mount St. Helens ranks as the most dangerously explosive volcano in the conterminous United States. The two employes of the US Geological Survey warned, "Eruption is likely within the next 100 years, possibly before the end of this century."

How right they were.

Thus it was really no surprise to earth scientists—although to everyone else it seemed a surprise—that Mount St. Helens began a vivid display of its cranky personality on March 27, 1980. And then, on May 18, 1980, when one whole side of the mountain was blown away in a massively explosive eruption, the rest of the world was awakened to the true nature of the forces that shaped the landscape of this geologically young and volcanically active region.

The Mullineaux-Crandell warning had been based, of course, on what they had been able to find out about the relatively recent geological history of the mountain. This is their description of the mountain and its history:

Mount St. Helens is a symmetrical volcanic cone in southwestern Washington about 45 miles northeast of Portland, Oregon. Most of the cone that can be seen now was formed within the last 1,000 years. But this overlies an older volcanic center that probably has existed for at least 40,000 years.

Mount St. Helens has had a long history of spasmodic explosive activity. We believe that it is an especially dangerous volcano because of its past behavior and its eruptions during the past 4,500 years.

Crandell and Mullineaux noted, too, that future eruptions will probably produce lava flows, volcanic domes, tephra (meaning pumice and other airborne debris), pyroclastic flows, and mud-flows. A pyroclastic flow is an explosively erupted, turbulent mixture of hot gases carrying volcanic fragments, crystals, ash, and glass shards. This broiling mass may come rolling down the side of the volcano at up to 100 miles (160 kilometers) an hour, burning and burying everything in its path.

Explaining their observations and their predictions, Crandell and Mullineaux wrote,

The nature of these future eruptions and the types of rocks produced will depend on the kinds of molten magma that move into the volcano. Three kinds of volcanic rock have been produced during past eruptions: basalt, andesite, and dacite. These rocks differ in chemical composition, particularly in the percentage of silicon dioxide (silica) they contain.

The chemical composition and gas content of the magma largely determine the manner in which it will be erupted. In general, basalt magma—lowest in silica content—is relatively fluid and tends to be erupted nonexplosively to form lava flows. Highly explosive eruptions of basalt are uncommon because gas escapes relatively easily from such magma.

However, dacite magma—highest in silica content—is relatively viscous, and gases do not readily escape from it. The initial eruption of gas-rich dacite is commonly explosive and forms pumice; domes are often formed in the closing stages of such an eruption. The behavior of andesite is intermediate between the characteristics of basalt and dacite.

While earth scientists are generally aware of the important differences between types of lavas, and the results of those differences, many people—conditioned by films and television programs showing syrup-thin lava running down hillsides—are unaware of such subtleties. Indeed, when Mount St. Helens erupted one of the most frequent questions from the public was "When will we see the lava?" Laymen seem to expect all volcanoes to act like Hawaii's Mauna Loa, producing hot ribbons of molten rock that go running down the mountain's flanks.

But that behavior is not typical of volcanoes like Mount St. Helens, which go through what are referred to as Peléan eruptions. Rather than rich flows of lava, Peléan type eruptions tend to produce pumice and talcum-fine ash particles that are exploded into the air when trapped gases are violently released.

Actually, in most such eruptions a flow of lava appears only after the eruption has been under way for some time, perhaps for days, weeks, or even months. Semirunny flows of lava, if they appear at all, may eventually be erupted from vents at the summit, or they can break through weak zones in the mountain's flanks. These flows, however, Crandell and Mullineaux said, seldom move more than 3 miles (5 kilometers) from the base of the volcano. The fronts of such lava flows tend to move quite slowly, perhaps as fast as a walking pace, or even at a rate that is barely noticeable. Even though slow, however, these flows are dangerous as they gradually creep up on stands of timber or buildings, starting fires and then burying the remains.

One of the things volcanologists expected, too, was that Mount St. Helens would begin building a new lava dome in the crater after the first series of eruptions. The volcano gradually forms a mushroom-shaped cap in the bottom of the crater as viscous, toothpaste-thick lava is extruded up through the vent from below. On occasion, however, the new dome can be explosively blown away by the next episode of eruptive activity.

It should be realized, of course, that the Mount St. Helens eruption of 1980—and the activity that followed—is a repeat performance of the many eruptive episodes discernible in the volcano's history. Indeed, Crandell and Mullineaux, in their research on the mountain, have been able to trace the volcano's activity back to about 2500 B.C., when it apparently erupted after a dormant period of some 4,000 years.

Through use of radioactive-dating techniques—using samples of ancient carbon from plant life buried in the debris—and other important clues, these researchers found evidence for perhaps 23 eruptions of Mount St. Helens in the past 4,500 years. These eruptions can be grouped roughly into four main periods: from

2500 B.C. to about 1600 B.C.; from 1200 B.C. to 800 B.C.; from 400 B.C. to 400 A.D.; and from 1300 A.D. to about 1850 A.D. And, the last tephra eruption prior to 1980 occurred in 1857.

The most recent eruptive episodes—excluding the 1980 eruption—involved four periods of activity clustered around the mid-nineteenth century. They were marked by eruptions of tephra, and lava flows were reported being seen before a dome eventually formed.

Previous to that, about 1800, an eruption occurred that marked the end of a dormant period of about 150 years. Since about 2500 B.C., Mount St. Helens's periods of dormancy have often been quite brief—some being only tens of years long—while others have lasted for 500 years or more.

What this says, of course, is that since 2500 B.C., Mount St. Helens has never been dormant for more than five centuries, and dormant periods of only one or two centuries have been more typical.

There are, of course, other views about Mount St. Helens and the eruption. Roy Wilson, chairman of the Cowlitz Tribe of northwest Indians, for example, wrote this for the Portland *Oregonian*:

My people, the Cowlitz Indians, were very close to our mountain, both physically and spiritually. The Cowlitz hunted, fished and lived at the base of the mountain, and it was known to be "their mountain."

Mountains are great persons to our Indian people. Mt. St. Helens has always been known to the Cowlitz Indians as Lawelatla (Person from Whom Smoke Comes). Each time the mountain rumbled and belched smoke it was speaking to our people. Indians have great respect for Mother Earth and every living thing. . . .

What do our people feel today as they hear their mountain speaking? Many of them believe that the present eruptions are an expression of spiritual powers contained in the mountain. A large number of our dead ancestors have been buried there, and white men, people of no morals or conscience, have desecrated their graves by digging them up. . . .

Some of our people believe the present eruptions are the spirits of our departed ancestors, rising up in divine retribution against these menacing white invaders.

The northwest Indians also developed some interesting legends that help explain Mount St. Helens's activity, its location and that of neighboring mountains. According to research done by Beatrice Buzzetti, one of these Indian legends held that a wrinkled old witch, Loowit (Loo-wit-lat-kla, Lady of Fire), faithfully kept the Sacred Fire, the only fire in the world, on a bridge—the Tamanous Bridge—that crossed the Columbia River. Indians from all directions came to that bridge to borrow fire, and because of her faithfulness and goodness, the Great Chief granted her the gift of eternal life. This gift had been granted to only a few others, including the Great Spirit's two sons, Klickitat and Wyeast.

Legends say that Loowit, however, was unhappy, weeping because she did not want to live forever as an ugly old crone. The Great Spirit, unable to rescind the grant of eternal life, then asked Loowit to name her greatest wish, and her request to be young and beautiful was granted.

Unfortunately, the legends say, both Wyeast and Klickitat fell in love with Loowit, and when she was unable to choose between them they fought, burning villages and forests in the process. The Great Spirit then frowned in righteous wrath, broke down the Tamanous Bridge, and killed the three lovers. Because he loved them, however, he raised a mighty mountain where each one fell.

"Because Loowit was beautiful, the mountain (Mount St. Helens) is (or was) a perfectly symmetrical cone, dazzling white," Miss Buzzetti wrote. "Young Wyeast (Mount Hood) lifts his head in pride. But Klickitat (Mount Adams), for all his rough ways, had a tender heart and wept to see the beautiful maiden wrapped in snow. So he bends his head forever in sorrow as he gazes down on Loowit in her beauty."

In all such legends, Miss Buzzetti said, Mount St. Helens is pictured as feminine, a maiden, her alluring curves the most graceful and symmetrical of all the Cascade volcanoes.

She also contended that because of the volcanic activity in these mountains, the local Indians, "even half-civilized Indians, cannot be induced—by hope or reward or fear of punishments—to approach their summits. Spirit Lake (on the flank of Mount St. Helens) is so named because the Indians believe that the entire region belongs to the dead and is the residence of 'devils' cast out from other tribes."

Such lore, she noted, is attributed to the sounds of air currents heard at Spirit Lake. And the large fish in the lake are said to be the spirits of warriors who have taken on that form as a way to jeer at fellow Indians who allowed white settlers to take over their territory.

Another Indian legend involves large hairy apelike creatures that supposedly inhabit the area around Mount St. Helens. This story apparently arose late, in about 1924, when a miner, Marion Smith, and five companions came down off the mountain reporting being attacked by a band of mysterious mountain apemen. One of these creatures was thought to have been killed by gunfire from the miners, and his body supposedly rolled off a cliff into a deep ravine, known appropriately as Ape Canyon. Search parties, however, found no clues whatever.

Nonetheless, given the legend, some enterprising prankster made a large footlike device that makes beautiful impressions in mud, and the legend has been kept alive, even by footprints from a monster with no left foot.

The Indians, of course, were the first human occupants of this region of North America. It was not until 1792 that their mountain, Lawelatla, was discovered by Captain George Vancouver, who, in October of that year, named it Mount St. Helens in honor of England's ambassador to the court of Madrid, British diplomat Alleyne Fitzherbert, Baron St. Helens.

While he was ambassador to Madrid in 1790, Fitzherbert had settled a dispute with the Spanish, thereby preserving the rights of British traders to do business at Nootka Sound, on the island that now bears Vancouver's name.

For making that settlement, Fitzherbert was given a peerage by the British crown. Vancouver, incidentally, also named a second peak in what is now Washington State after his third lieutenant, Joseph Baker, and two other peaks—Hood and Rainier—after admirals then serving with the British Navy.

The first ascent of Mount St. Helens by white adventurers was made by a party headed by Thomas J. Dreyer, in 1853, while the volcano was in an eruptive phase. Dreyer, the first editor of the Portland *Oregonian*, led a party on a 2 week trip to the base of Mount St. Helens, up to the top to view the smoking crater, and then home again.

"The higher we ascended, the more difficult our progress," he wrote. "The atmosphere produced a singular affect [sic] upon all the parties. Each face looked pale and sallow. And all complained of a strange ringing in the ears. It appeared as if there were hundreds of fine-toned bells ringing in our ears. Blood started from our noses and all of us found respiration difficult."

Dreyer's party also reported that the crater, which had been reported to be on the mountain's southwest side, was actually on the northwest side. Smoke was continually spewing from the crater's mouth, and it is probable that the physical effects Dreyer's party experienced were related to the sulfur-laden gases issuing from the crater.

Since then, certainly, thousands of hikers have worked their way to the top of the mountain to take in the peak's spectacular view of the Northwest, including the peaks of Mount Adams, Mount Hood, and Mount Rainier.

Although it is obvious that Mount St. Helens is quite young in geological terms, the first really documented activity on the 9,677-foot (2,950-meter) peak came from missionaries in the Northwest who witnessed a number of large eruptions beginning in 1842. They wrote of violent events that produced ash deposits at The Dalles and killed fish in the Toutle River. Also, that series of eruptions produced the first recorded casualty of volcanic activity from Mount St. Helens: an Indian deer hunter who suffered severe burns on his foot and leg when he tried to leap across a lava flow.

Reports from that time also indicate there were at least three distinct vents spewing steam, ash, and gases from different sides of the peak. And it was one of these vents that eventually extruded the domelike feature known as Goat Rocks. It was the Goat Rocks area, too, that was swelling outward so rapidly just before the most recent massive explosion on May 18, 1980. Another of those earlier events was apparently associated with formation of what was called the Forsyth Bulge.

The series of volcanic events in the last century began in earnest with an eruption of tephra and ash on November 22, 1842. The volcano then entered its most violent phase the next month, in

December. This episode was followed by repeated, more moderate eruptions that continued into 1844. By 1847 it was reported that the dacite dome making up the Goat Rocks formation had been emplaced and was cooling. In all, this activity continued sporadically until 1857.

No records of these events were left by the traders of the Hudson's Bay Company, but fortunately some missionaries—especially Josiah Lamberson Parrish (1806–1895)—were in the area to witness the events and write down their impressions.

Parrish, stationed at the Methodist mission at Champoeg, French Prairie, on the lower Willamette River, observed on November 23, 1842, that Mount St. Helens had "changed her snowy dress of pure white for a sombre black mantle, which she wore until the snows of the ensuing winter fell upon her."

Parrish also reported that "the ashes fell at The Dalles to the depth of half an inch, so I was informed by the missionaries stationed there. The eruption was on the south side of the mountain, about two-thirds of the distance from the bottom to the top. I had occasion to pass down the river (the Columbia) about a year or two after the eruption, and could still see distinctly the fire burning upon the side of the mountain."

In a later report, Parrish's observations were reported in an 1885 issue of the *Morning Oregonian*, in Portland. That article read, in part,

The mountain seemed to belch forth great masses of smoke and vapor. White puffs of steam rose like columns of scrollwork to the very mid-heavens, constantly changing and assuming new forms upon the sky.

Vast quantities of organic matter [actually probably ash] were erupted; ashes and rocks were thrown out with tremendous force, but no noise was heard at that distance. Strata of color lay on the horizon, varying from inky blackness to white puffs of steam that assumed a thousand fantastic shapes.

Lava ran into the near branches of the Cowlitz, perhaps five miles away, that heated the water and killed many fishes—so old settlers on that river said. . . .

Flames were seen for a long time issuing from a crater on the south side of the mountain, two-thirds of the way up. He was at Clatsop in 1843, and saw fires burning there.

Another Methodist missionary, Gustavus Hines (1809–1873), wrote in his document *A Voyage round the World: With a History of the Oregon Mission* that Mount St. Helens "was discovered, all at once, to be covered with a dense cloud of smoke."

"When the first volumes of smoke had passed away," he added, "it could be seen, from various parts of the country, that an eruption had taken place on the north side of St. Helen's [sic], a little below the summit, and from the smoke that continued to issue from the chasm or crater, it was pronounced to be a volcano in active operation."

After commenting on the spread of ashes downwind in amounts "so as to admit of its being collected in quantities," Hines remarked that the eruption "has led many to suppose that volcanic eruptions are not uncommon in this country."

A Catholic missionary, Jean Baptiste Zacharie Bolduc, was northwest of Mount St. Helens, occupying the mission of St. Francis on the lower Cowlitz River, when he witnessed an eruption on December 5, 1842. He reported that the eruption caused a fish kill in what is now the Toutle River, and he provided confirmation of the report that a vent had appeared on the north or northwest side of the mountain. It was Bolduc, indeed, who reported seeing three active vents on the mountain.

What Bolduc was witnessing, apparently, was the period of most intense activity on the mountain between the eruption that began in November, 1842, and the massive explosion that tore one whole side off the mountain in 1980.

An unidentified French-Canadian fur trapper, who apparently lived some 20 miles (32 kilometers) from Mount St. Helens, told geologist Samuel Franklin Emmons that "the light from the burning volcano was so intense that one could see to pick up a pin in the grass at midnight near his cabin, which is some 20 miles (30 kilometers) distant in a straight line."

In later years, after 1857, when the last tephra eruption occurred, the evidence of the midnineteenth-century eruption was gradually eliminated by erosion or covered by ice and snow. In 1860, for example, a climbing party reported it could still see a crater on the north side of the mountain, "a plainly visible yawning crater—now cold as the snow around it." That crater apparently became covered later by ice and snow, possibly beneath part of the Forsyth glacier.

Some reports from climbing parties indicate that the northwest crater probably cooled enough by 1883 so that it did become buried beneath glacial ice. By then, all that could be found of the once violent volcanic activity were some minor fumaroles near a formation called The Boot.

The 1860 climbing party also reported, however, that while descending on the southwest side of Mount St. Helens they found an unusual system of crevasses that seemed to be emitting steam. This, then, might have been what was left of the once active vent reported on that side of the mountain.

Several exploratory parties later looked for evidence of a south, west, or southwest vent, but their reports are conflicting. Indeed, as late as 1917 it was reported that a fumarole site had been seen on the southwest side of the Mount St. Helens peak, just below the summit. This report came from members of a work crew hauling materials to the summit to build a lookout house.

Much later, in 1971, indeed, radiometric observations of the south side of Mount St. Helens showed what was described by Jules D. Friedman and David G. Frank, both of the US Geological Survey, as a "bright anomaly," meaning it was considerably warmer when viewed by infrared heat detectors than the surrounding terrain. A year later, however, it was only seen as a "dim anomaly."

At that time, 1972, however, field teams observed that the warm area consisted of "five linear warm zones that extend down a talus slope. The warm ground is adjacent to two small remnants of stubby lava flows, near the contact between the summit dacite dome and the sliderock of the talus slope." Evidence was also found for a few small vents that had probably carried vapor through the rubble.

After the major eruption of May 18, 1980, of course, such questions are essentially moot. Now much of the terrain on the mountain's flanks has been covered by a cascade of debris from the area of the crater, plus a fresh surface of fine ash. And as study

Infrared thermograph taken in December 1975, showing the location of a fumarole area on the mountain's southwest flank. The triple junction of rock outcrops lies just south of the mountain's summit. (Oregon Army National Guard image)

continues, scientists will be probing for new patterns of heat flow, for "bright anomalies," that may yield hints about what is going on underground.

What should be clear by now, certainly, is that we have all seen, first hand, how Mount St. Helens earned its reputation as a particularly active, explosively eruptive volcano. And it should also be clear that Mount St. Helens is not alone; it is merely one of the 14 large volcanoes that helped create the beautiful terrain that makes up the Pacific Northwest.

Technical Vignette:
Side-looking airborne
radar: SLAR
Charles Rosenfeld

The often cloud-covered landscape of the Pacific Northwest has provided an excellent test for the usefulness of cloud-penetrating mapping systems such as side-looking airborne radar (SLAR). Long before the eruption of Mount St. Helens in 1980, such radar imaging was being used for assessment of volcanic hazards by mapping the size of the massive prehistoric mudflows (lahars) associated with several Cascade volcanoes and by giving structural geologists insight into the tectonic fabric of the Cascade Range.

Indeed, in 1978 the imaging radar aboard the ill-fated SEASAT satellite had produced a very clear picture of Mount St. Helens and the Portland, Oregon, area, as taken from orbit high above earth's atmosphere. The extent of the former lahars from Mount St. Helens stood out clearly as a smooth blanket filling the valleys of an otherwise rough landscape. Then the failure of the satellite's power supply—after only 99 days of operation—terminated what was proving to be a valuable reconnaissance tool.

As for Mount St. Helens, soon after the first swarm of small earthquakes was detected beneath the mountain on March 20, the Oregon Army National Guard's SLAR-equipped OV-1 Mohawk aircraft were used to fly radar coverage of the area. The idea was to locate the portions of the area's tectonic fabric that were affected by the apparent motion that was causing the earthquakes under the mountain. Early analysis of the seismic epicenters indicated that a right-lateral strike-slip motion was occurring along a line trending from Mount Margaret south through the center of Mount St. Helens's volcanic cone.

Although no direct surface expression of this motion was detected in the SLAR images, other faults and lineaments were clearly visible.

The most exciting results from SLAR imaging came immediately after the massive explosion of the mountain on May 18. Initial observations near the tall ash plume indicated that the plume was boiling up out of the north flank of the crater. But because of the density of the plume, visual observations could not determine whether the north flank had actually been blasted away or was merely hidden beneath the rising plume and the cascade of pyroclastic flows.

That question was quite quickly answered by the SLAR equipment carried aboard the National Guard's Mohawk aircraft. The instrument's X-band (3-cm wavelength) microwaves easily penetrated all but the densest part of the ash column, and the fixed-target returns clearly showed the volcanic vent and the outline of the crater. The crater appeared to be so large, indeed, that a second SLAR run was made just to confirm the scene for the aircraft crew, who found it hard to believe. At the same time, the instrument's moving target returns provided a map of the heavily ash-laden core of the volcanic plume and also detected the movement of the large mudflows that were sliding down the adjacent river valleys. So successful was that initial pass at imaging the breached crater that the Mohawks were asked to maintain a constant SLAR vigil until 6 A.M. the next day.

During the series of subsequent eruptions, too, the SLAR instrument has been exceptionally valuable, especially when cloud cover or darkness has obscured visual observations. Because the SLAR equipment was available, the eruptions of May 25, June 12, and August 7 were especially well studied.

In addition to the Mohawk-borne instrument, further radar coverage of the Mount St. Helens area was made by two experimental systems operated by the National Aeronautics and Space Administration (NASA). One of these systems was carried aboard a Convair 880 jetliner, while the other was carried by a high-flying B-57 research plane. Both instruments were what are called synthetic aperture radar systems, and the data they collect requires computer processing after the aircraft land. These systems provide better resolution than the SLAR equipment aboard the Mohawks, but the SLAR instruments yield their results immediately.

Other data important for study of the eruptions were collected by weather radar and air traffic control radar systems in Portland, Oregon. These systems helped in tracking the volcanic plumes as they ascended into the stratosphere, as well as when the plumes began drifting downwind.

With these results, it has become obvious that data collected via radar have provided much more information than would have been gathered only visually. It indicates that radar—even radar from space—should become a powerful means for monitoring volcanic eruptions in the future.

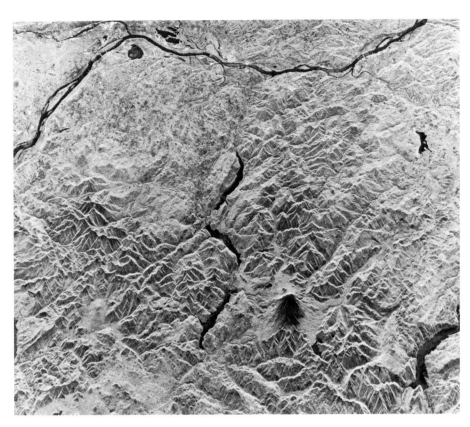

Synthetic-aperture radar (SAR) image from the SEASAT satellite. Image taken from earth orbit on August 13, 1978.

Side-looking airborne radar (SLAR) was used to penetrate, or look through, the heavy plume of smoke and ash coming from Mount St. Helens on May 18, 1980. The image is divided into two channels, with the top using a fixed-target mode to illustrate stationary objects, the moving target mode emphasizing motion by measuring Doppler shift. The fixed-target mode shows the outline of the newly formed explosion crater and the mudflows entering the valleys. The moving target mode shows the eruption plume boiling up out of the crater. The aircraft that took the images was 6 miles (10 kilometers) west of the mountain at an altitude of 18,500 feet (5,600 meters).

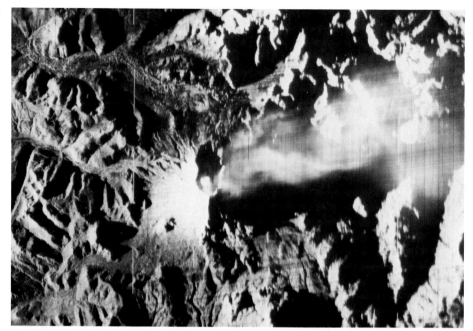

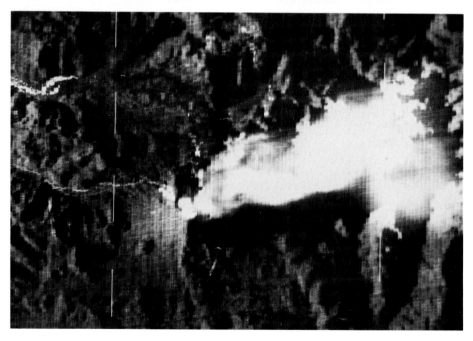

Above:
X-band (3 centimeter wavelength) SLAR image acquired on June 14, 1980, while the first dacitic dome was being extruded into the crater.

Right:
A B-57 aircraft operated by the National Aeronautics and Space Administration was flying at 12 miles (19 kilometers) altitude to acquire this SAR image showing the June dome in the center of the crater. (NASA image, courtesy of Roger Arno, Ames Research Center)

4 | *One Worldwide System*

Maybe it was just coincidence, but when a series of large earthquakes rumbled through California's high Sierra Nevada—close to the time when Mount St. Helens, 600 miles (950 kilometers) to the north, began pouring ash and gas into the sky—worriers immediately asked the obvious: "What's the connection?"

There is, unfortunately, no obvious mechanism to connect volcanic hiccups in one place with seismic shivers elsewhere. At the same time, however, both the volcano in Washington State and the system of earthquake faults that dominates California's landscape are indeed active, important parts of a single worldwide system that has made the earth's crust what it is today. So they are, indeed, connected—by being offspring of this single worldwide system—but they are not known to be mutually triggered.

Scientists involved in studies of the earth's crust and its evolution call this idea of a worldwide system the theory of plate tectonics. This theory was proposed by German geophysicist Alfred L. Wegener in 1912, who held that all the earth's continents originated in a single land mass in the Carboniferous era, then split and drifted apart to take up their present positions.

Over the years this theory gradually became accepted among European geophysicists, but their American counterparts remained unconvinced until only recently, since the 1950s. Wegener's idea is rather widely accepted now because the evidence has become convincingly solid. Indeed, the theory of plate tectonics supplies both a unifying and satisfying explanation for much of the geological activity observed in the earth's crust. This theory holds, basically, that all of the earth's crust is broken up into perhaps seven major plates—and a dozen or more smaller plates—which constantly rub, bump, and grind against each other as they jostle for position. Such activity—the bumping and grinding of crustal plates—provides the fuel for volcanoes and supplies the energy for earthquakes.

In addition, some of the major plates appear to be growing by adding new, young material to one border, along what are called seafloor spreading centers. As the new material is added, however, the plates are apparently being shoved aside and collide violently with plates at the other end.

Plate tectonics map of the world, azimuthal equidistant projection centered on the Pacific Northwest. (Compiled and drawn by Linda M. Donaldson.)

Legend: —, midoceanic ridges (spreading centers); ⋯, oceanic trenches (subduction zones); —, transverse fracture zones; ---, uncertain plate boundaries. Plates: 1, Australian; 2, Philippine; 3, Caroline; 4, Bismarck; 5, Fiji; 6, Pacific; 7, Eurasian; 8, North American; 9, Juan de Fuca; 10, Cocos; 11, Caribbean; 12, Nazca; 13, South American; 14, Scotia; 15, Sandwich; 16, Iranian; 17, Arabian; 18, Turkish; 19, Aegean; 20, Adriatic; 21, African; 22, Somali; 23, Antarctic.

Major active volcanoes of the world (dots).

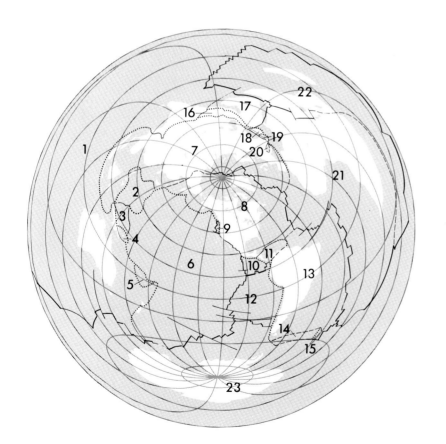

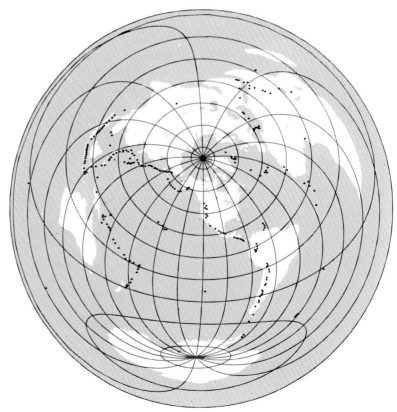

"The theory of plate tectonics provides a basis for speculation that the Mount St. Helens eruption and the California earthquakes may be indirectly related," said Roy Bailey, a volcanologist at the US Geological Survey's headquarters in Reston, Virginia.

But despite this connection, Bailey said, "the direct geological link between the two events—which are 600 miles (950 kilometers) apart—is tenuous at best."

Nonetheless, the coincidence was too good to pass up, and geophysicist Don Anderson, at the California Institute of Technology, in Pasadena, decided it was worth doing some research into historic records.

"This new eruption brought interest to bear on the previous eruption," Anderson explained. "So I started looking around in the records." He found that "in 1857, not only were Mount St. Helens and Mount Lassen erupting, but—in 1858 and 1859—Mount Rainier and Mount Baker also showed activity."

It was also in 1857, Anderson said, that a great earthquake—estimated at 8 or more on the Richter scale of magnitude—struck the Los Angeles area of southern California.

"In 1857 a volcano in Baja California (Mexico), Tres Virgines, also erupted," Anderson said. "So we have a coincidence of a volcano in Baja California and several in the Cascades erupting about the same time as the big earthquake occurred in southern California."

He also found in the records that "The next big earthquake in southern California (in 1870) was the Owens Valley earthquake, which was probably the biggest earthquake felt there in the past several hundred years." During the years surrounding that large event, he said, there were major volcanic eruptions of the Sierra de San Andreas and Mount Colima volcanoes in Mexico. And, in Washington State, Mount Rainier and Mount Baker were again showing signs of activity.

Going farther back, however, the historical record becomes quite fuzzy. Still, some older reports suggest there was a major earthquake along California's notorious San Andreas fault in 1845. In that same period, a volcano erupted in British Columbia, Canada, and the Tres Virgines volcano was active in Baja California.

"So we again have a coincidence in time, with the volcanoes in the Cascades and in Mexico erupting at about the same time as a large earthquake in southern California. But the date of that earthquake is more uncertain then [the dates] for the volcanoes," Anderson explained.

In this century, too, similar patterns of earthquake and volcanic activity have been seen, in about 1915 and again in 1940. "In 1915 and 1940," Anderson said, "there were sequences of earthquakes in the Imperial Valley (of southern California), in the Mojave Desert, in the Mammoth Lakes area, and in Mexico, near the northern end of the Gulf of California. And there was also some volcanic activity in 1913 at Colima in Mexico, and from 1914 to 1917 Mount Lassen was erupting. In 1941 there were some questionable reports about Mount St. Helens and Colima showing activity."

And, from 1975 to 1980, in a period when both Mount Baker in Washington and Mount St. Helens have shown unmistakable activity, a series of large—but not great—earthquakes went rattling through California. In the fall of 1979, for instance, an earthquake measured at 6.4 on the Richter scale hit southern California, and the following spring—when Mount St. Helens was showing her cantankerous, explosive personality—some large temblors struck the Mammoth Lakes region near Bishop, California.

"The conclusion" then, Anderson said, "is that large earthquakes over a fairly large area occur coincidentally in time" along with volcanic activity. "So we can't look at earthquakes in southern California independently of plate tectonics and the activity of the whole system."

Bailey, arguing that such an idea remains far from solid, did comment that volcanic activity in the Pacific Northwest and earthquake activity in California could, conceivably, result from an episode of accelerated spreading along the midocean ridges. These ridges represent "sutures" between crustal plates—cracks marking the boundaries of adjacent plates on the seafloor—where the plates are being gradually pushed aside. Where they part, molten material from beneath the surface wells up and solidifies to build new oceanic crust, new seafloor. These are the midocean spreading centers.

Accelerated activity—faster spreading of the saefloor—along such a boundary, Bailey said, "could drive the northwestward-moving Pacific Plate in California and the eastward-moving Cascadia Plate (or Juan de Fuca Plate) in Washington and Oregon against the North American Plate with increased force, causing the two types of activity."

Even though that idea seems possible, however, Bailey warned that it is highly speculative. He added, "If the Cascade volcanoes are entering an episode of increased activity—as seems evident from recent events at Mount Baker, Mount Shasta, and Mount St. Helens—then the next few decades may provide a rare opportunity to detect such a relationship."

Anderson suggested, too, that the coincidences between earthquakes and volcanic eruptions might suggest that eruptions could serve as warnings of impending large earthquakes. He cautioned, however, that "it has not been demonstrated that there's a linkage between the earthquakes and volcanic activity." He said he looks on his historical research as only "a preliminary study to see whether volcanoes can, in any sense, act as a stress guage to warn that a large area (such as southern California) is ready to go."

As the statements by Anderson and Bailey suggest—and as the theory of plate tectonics requires—Mount St. Helens, the rest of the Cascade volcanoes, and the volcanoes in Mexico and Central America are all elements of what is called the Pacific Ring of Fire. Similarly, California's recurrent earthquakes represent another important link in this zone of activity, the Pacific Ring of Fire, which extends down through South America, around to New Zealand, up to Japan, and then through the Aleutian Islands and Alaska. These areas bordering the Pacific seafloor stand as the most violently active zone of seismic and volcanic tumult in the world.

As noted, all of these areas owe their unstable geological personalities to the fact that out in the Pacific Ocean the seafloor is splitting episodically along jagged seams, where seafloor spreading is occurring. On both sides of these seams, the massive crustal plates are slowly gliding away from each other, being shoved imperceptibly toward shore, toward the continents.

This finding, indeed, is the most fundamental geological discovery of this century. It has turned out—much to the surprise of many scientists—that the continental blocks and the ocean basins are completely different, both in terms of their structures and the materials of which they are made. No longer is it thought that the ocean basins are merely low-lying portions of a common crust that is just covered by water.

As this complex, sliding system evolves, collisions are, of course, inevitable. And where the seafloor slab crunches up against another slab, such as the North American Plate, something must yield. And, since the seafloor plates tend to be made of denser, heavier basaltic material, the lighter granitic continental plates appear able to ride up, overtopping the oceanic plates. This then forces the oceanic material to bend and drift downward, back into the earth's hot interior. This creates a so-called subduction zone, which is usually marked by those deep ocean trenches adjacent to the continents, or by island arcs such as the Japanese archipelago or the Aleutian Islands.

Theory also holds that as this descending plate reaches depths of about 200 miles (300 kilometers), it is gradually remelted—by both the earth's interior heat and the friction of being shoved down. As the rocks that make up the plate remelt in the denser medium of the earth's mantle, the material begins seeking cracks and fissures through which it can migrate toward the surface.

"If you've got some regional fault patterns, and some regional earthquakes that help open up the ground," said geologist Richard Birney, "they will allow the magma (the molten rock) to escape to the surface."

Birney, a faculty member at Dartmouth College in New Hampshire, said the result of such action—the presence of migrating magma and an active fault system—is production of a chain of volcanoes similar to the 14, including Mount St. Helens, seen in the Pacific Northwest. All of these Cascade volcanoes are associated with the subduction zone that apparently sends the Juan de Fuca Plate plunging beneath the North American continent, down to be melted and to supply new magma for the Cascade volcanoes.

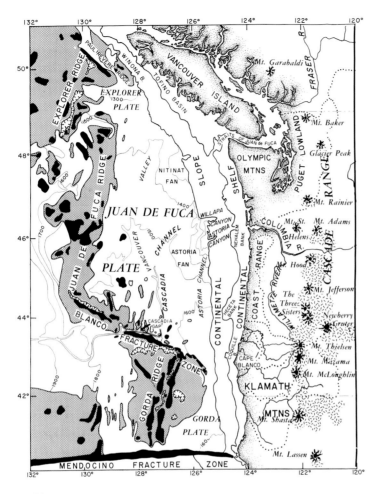

Map of the Pacific Northwest shows the relative positions of oceanic plates in relation to the continent and the Cascade volcanoes. (Compiled by Geologic Oceanography, Oregon State University)

Some recently gathered data now also suggest that two crustal plates—the Juan de Fuca and Farallon plates—began sliding beneath the North American Plate about 80 million years ago. Evidence suggests that this subduction event triggered the massive fissure eruptions that loosed floods of basaltic lava to flow across the land, creating the lava plains that formed in Oregon, Washington, and Idaho 60 million years ago.

As that episode ended, about 35 million years ago, an arc of offshore islands was created to the west, built from flowing basaltic lava released by a series of shield volcanoes similar to those in Hawaii. Since then, gradual erosion processes have modified the landforms and deposited large amounts of sediments.

Also, as subduction continued, some of these sedimentary materials were folded into what became the present Coast Range mountains, while more sediment was deposited to create the present continental shelf offshore.

While subduction activity proceeds, some of these sediments are carried down with the basaltic seafloor to be remelted at depth, and this mix of basalt and sedimentary rock yields the intermediate type of lava called andesite. The andesite, in general, is what has erupted to produce the high stratovolcanoes in the Cascade Range during the past million years.

An unusual feature of subduction in the Pacific Northwest, however, is the absence of a deep offshore trench. Subduction zones found along continental margins elsewhere—such as where the South American continent meets the subducting plate coming in from the Pacific Ocean—are marked by the presence of incredibly deep trenches. But no such trench exists off the coast of the Pacific Northwest, even though the magnetic signature of the seafloor seems to disappear there beneath the continental shelf.

A close study of this region of the Northwest coast has been conducted by Vern Kulm, of Oregon State University, since the early 1970s. Kulm, an oceanographer, has been looking at the edge of the continental shelf—the so-called continental slope—by doing borings, dredging, and seismic analysis. He has proposed, indeed, that progressively younger wedges of sediments have been thrust beneath the edge of the continental shelf as the small Juan de Fuca Plate continues being subducted. This pro-

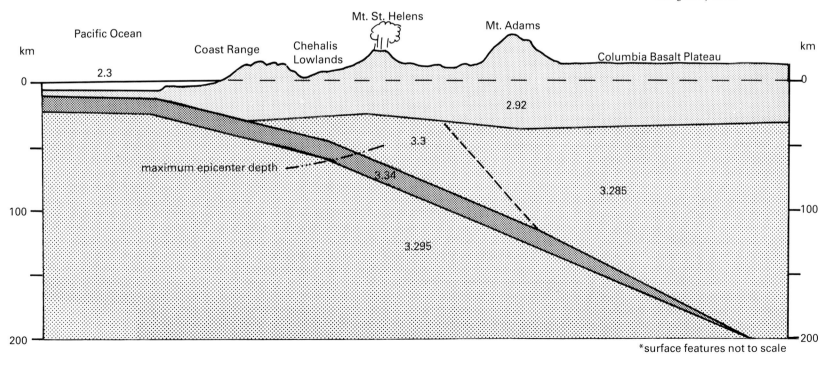

Cross section of the Pacific Northwest, showing subduction of the Juan de Fuca plate beneath the continental plate. The numbers represent inferred rock densities (in grams per cubic centimeter) modeled on the basis of seismic and gravity data.

Pacific Ocean

Mt. St. Helens

Mt. Adams

km

Coast Range

Chehalis
Lowlands

Columbia Basalt Plateau

km

2.3

0

0

2.92

3.3

maximum epicenter depth

3.34

3.285

100

100

3.295

200

200

*surface features not to scale

cess has apparently continued at a rate of about 2 inches (5 or 6 centimeters) per year for the past 10 million years. In addition, continuing, increasingly detailed analyses of heat flow, topography, gravity, and geology have left little doubt that the Juan de Fuca Plate is actively subducting.

A research geophysicist at Canada's Pacific Geoscience Center, Robin Riddihough, has also observed that while earthquakes—those of up to magnitude 6 on the Richter scale—frequently occur between the edge of the continental shelf and the volcanic Cascades, their epicenters never exceed depths of more than 43 miles (70 kilometers). This is thought to be true because earthquakes only occur in rigid plates, and below 43 miles (70 kilometers) the subducting plate is believed to become plastic, not capable of generating temblors.

From this work and extensive gravity data, then, Riddihough has inferred a model that calls for a thin plate, 12 miles (20 kilometers) thick, being subducted only a short distance from the spreading center where it is created. This small plate, too, is being remelted at depths of 43 miles (70 kilometers) or less. In essence, then, Riddihough proposes the Juan de Fuca Plate makes up a small closed system that has all of its boundaries, its zones of creation and destruction, contained within a few hundred kilometers.

If this scenario works out in detail, then the Juan de Fuca Plate may offer an almost ideal model for studying the dynamics of plate tectonics and the effects on volcanoes. With the existing concentration of geological and geophysical research institutions already in the Pacific Northwest, there is reason to hope that a total assessment of this small plate can be made. Such an assessment could result in an understanding of the plate's total energy budget, which is a summing of the release of seismic strain, vertical and horizontal movements, heat flow, and gravity effects. It seems possible that such a study of this one system could answer some of the fundamental questions about the nature of the plate-tectonics process and its still unknown driving force.

Mount St. Helens and the similar Cascade volcanoes, however, represent only one margin of this massive geological system. The so-called spreading centers on the seafloor represent the other margin, where researchers are only now finding a wonderland of geological and biological activity. The discoveries, indeed, are coming at such a pace, and are so startling, that both geologists and biologists are still trying to untangle all the ramifications.

The most exciting step in this series of discoveries came in 1977, when geologist Robert Ballard and his colleagues took the US Navy's deep-diving submersible *Alvin* 8,900 feet (2,800 meters) down to the bottom of the sea near the Galapagos Islands. There, at a place now known as the Galapagos spreading center, they found what they expected—spots where hot water was streaming from seafloor fissures. These hot springs are closely analogous to the hot springs and geysers known so well on land, but with important differences.

What they also found—but were not even prepared to expect—were rich colonies of strange creatures apparently living off geothermal energy supplied by the hotsprings. Indeed, these explorers may as well have visited another planet, because they had stumbled upon a whole new life-support system based on dissolved sulfur compounds. There it was: life in the dark, life without photosynthesis.

Ballard, from the Woods Hole Oceanographic Institution, found the geology interesting because it confirmed that hot springs do form in these deep-sea fissures at the crustal spreading centers. But most attention focused quickly on the creatures inhabiting these geothermally warmed zones on the seafloor. There were tube worms, stranger tube worms than had ever been seen before, growing inside Nylon-like tubes that were as much as 10 feet (3 meters) long. At the top ends of these whitish tubes were the vivid-red heads of the worms waving in the sea, apparently somehow collecting food—or energy—from the warmed water.

"We're still high on this whole thing," said George Somero, a marine biologist at the Scripps Institute of Oceanography in La Jolla, California. "Every time we look we find something new and unusual. Every day we think of something new we can do."

And the tube worms, he said, "are just the beginning."

Somero, who has been studying how these long tube worms live, said that "it looks as if the sea worms are chemical autotrophs—meaning they use inorganics [inorganic chemicals such as sulfur, nitrogen, or oxygen] to get their energy for life." Indeed it is possible, he said, that the worms could be taking sulfide compounds directly from seawater to make one of life's most important energy chemicals, ATP (adenosinetriphosphate).

Still, Somero added, these worms may make use of bacteria that live inside their bright red bodies and turn the inorganic molecules into organic chemicals that the worms can use for metabolism. But this was yet to be decided. Even so, Somero said, "this is essentially unheard of in the animal kingdom."

This research work also led to the discovery—by Somero and his colleagues—that these worms contain special enzymes that are normally involved in a chemical reaction pathway known as the Calvin-Benson cycle. This is a process that green plants—and some bacteria—use in photosynthesis.

"So what the worm is able to do is fix carbon dioxide much the same as a plant can. And the levels of these key enzymes are equivalent to about what you might find in a green vegetable leaf, such as spinach."

Another scientist who specializes in doing research on marine worms—Dr. Meredith Jones, at the Smithsonian Institution in Washington, DC—has remarked that the physical structure of these 10-foot-long seaworms is also unusual. What this discovery on the deep seafloor amounts to, he said, is "fitting another block into our knowledge of the diversity of life. In working with marine worms, you see what you think are all the possible permutations and combinations" of structure. But after receiving these newly discovered worms to study, he added "I just sort of sat back and said, 'My God, there is a different way to put them together; there is a different way to live.' I started out with a rather blasé attitude—since I'm used to seeing all these other worms—but then you realize you don't know it all."

Actually, finding all that new biology—living off volcanic energy—was exciting enough, but in April of 1979 Ballard and his colleagues struck a true geological bonanza. Using *Alvin*, diving to the bottom at a location now known as 21 Degrees North, off the western coast of Mexico, they found a spot where hot springs are much more active, where super-heated plumes of seawater are being shot straight up out of meters-tall chimneys on the seafloor.

These chimneys were named "white smokers" or "black smokers," depending on the color of the plumes streaming from them. And, as the scientists maneuvered tiny *Alvin* close so they could test the temperature of the water rushing from the chimneys, the water turned out to be so hot that their plastic temperature probe melted. On a later expedition, however, more rugged instruments recorded the plume temperatures at more than 660°F (350°C). Some samples of that mineral-rich water were also taken for analysis.

Since then, too, another group of oceanographers—J. B. Corliss, J. A. Baross, and S. E. Hoffman, at Oregon State University—have proposed that similar undersea hotsprings in the ancient, primordial seas may indeed have been where life originated. In a report delivered at the annual meeting of the American Geophysical Union in December 1980, they stated,

A diverse set of observations of Archean fossil-bearing rocks, modern submarine hydrothermal systems, experimental and theoretical work on the abiotic synthesis of organic molecules and primitive organized structures, and on water-rock interactions, suggest that submarine hot springs were the site for synthesis of organic compounds leading to the first living organisms on earth.

They noted that such hydrothermal systems include large flows of heat energy under highly reducing conditions, have abundant and appropriate catalytic surface areas such as clay minerals, and have sufficient concentrations of the right organic chemicals.

The continuous flow of hot water through the system, they added, "removes products from the site of reaction upward through a mixing gradient of temperature and composition."

This Oregon State University team then suggested that a sequence of reactions beginning with methane, ammonia, and molecular hydrogen might have led to the gradual formation of amino acids, then proteins, complex polymers, organized structures capable of metabolism, and on to living, reproducing organisms.

They went on to suggest, too, that microorganisms found in the carefully preserved samples from sulfide chimneys taken from the East Pacific Rise at the 21 Degrees North site "may be modern counterparts of Archean fossil organisms."

It is a startling idea that the huge system responsible for much of the earth's geology is also intimately involved in supplying the undersea incubators for life itself, and that the process may still be continuing. Much work, of course, still needs to be done, but the idea should spark a lot of new work in that direction.

These findings at the 21 Degree North location, according to Ballard and John Edmond, have probably also changed our whole understanding of the sea and its chemistry. What they found was strong evidence that a dynamic system—powered by the same energy that caused Mount St. Helens's massive eruption—is at work recycling all the water of the world's oceans.

In a possibly related discovery, an ecological research team from Oregon State University uncovered species of microorganisms from the underside of rocks surrounding steam vents on the lava dome in the Mount St. Helens crater. These organisms formed a filamentaceous trail in condensing steam at 208°F (98°C). According to John Baross and Cliff Dahm, research assistant professors with the OSU team, the crater organisms appear to be physically and metabolically similar to certain species collected at the 21 Degree North site. But whether such organisms are carried by hot ground water systems connected to the sea or arrived by other means is yet unknown.

It has become apparent through this work that all the water in the seas is flowing constantly, on a massive scale, through this underground "pressure-cooker" system, and that this flow is helping to maintain the sea's chemical balance. Indeed, the system is responsible for laying down some of the world's richest mineral deposits.

Because of these possibilities, some scientists are calling this the discovery of a lifetime, and John Edmond, from the Massachusetts Institute of Technology, believes it is at least the discovery of the decade.

What is certain, of course, is that this discovery can provide an exciting new understanding of the oceans, their history, and their chemistry. It is painting a picture of the sea very different from what scientists thought they knew. Among the surprises are these:

All the water in the oceans may be recycled through this hot pressure-cooker system every 8 million years, strongly controlling the sea's salinity. That may seem slow, but in the oceans' lifetime of 3.5 billion years, that is enough to recycle the seas more than 400 times.

There are large bodies of rich metallic ores—the seafloor chimneys and fallout from the hot plumes—in the process of being formed. It is now known where these ores come from, how fast they can be formed, and how such strange deposits originate. Such knowledge may even lead to new ideas about where to look for such rich deposits on land.

These seafloor hotsprings may play a role in controlling the sea's chemistry equal to that of all the rivers and streams—large and small—that pour constantly into the sea. This discovery should help balance the equation for the amount of minerals dissolved in the sea.

While only a few areas having active undersea hotsprings have been studied so far, the scientists involved suspect that many similar zones of geothermal activity exist along the 30,000 miles (48,000 kilometers) of the midocean-ridge system, the spreading centers. This system is known to wind its way through all the oceans on the globe, rather like the seam that meanders around a baseball.

Edmond, in an interview, explained that "associated with this spreading of the seafloor are essentially submarine volcanoes." But, unlike Mount St. Helens, which expends its energy by tossing ash, steam, and gas into the air, in these seafloor vents "essentially half of the heat (energy) is transported hydrothermally" by water flowing through the cracks and fissures. This water, having infiltrated into the faults and cracks, sets up circulation patterns underground as it is heated to high temperature by the rocks. "But you don't get the explosive kinds of effects associated with (land surface) vulcanism," Edmond elaborated, because at ocean depths of 9,300 feet (2,800 meters) "the pressure prevents the water from boiling."

One of the important points to remember, he added, is that when this superheated water contacts the hot rocks underground, the water "gets changed dramatically; it becomes very acidic. It then extracts a large number of metals from the basalt, such as iron, manganese, copper, zinc, silver, lead, and others. The other important thing is that the scale of this activity is so enormous that it has a large effect on the chemistry of seawater itself."

In the past, he explained, "the classical idea was that the chemistry of the oceans was due to the transport of stuff from the continents into the holding tank, the sea." It was also thought that these minerals are removed from the ocean water when they precipitate out to become seafloor sediments.

But there were some serious problems with that idea. It wasn't clear how the ocean could maintain itself, how it could keep from becoming a very salty, very alkaline thing like Utah's Great Salt Lake, or the Dead Sea.

What happens, when you look at the amount of heat involved, at the temperature of the water, is that you can calculate the flow rates, the amount of water you have to have to do the job for you every year. It turns out to be one half of 1 percent of the amount of water coming (into the sea) from all the rivers. That translates into pumping—or cycling through this high temperature zone—a volume of water equivalent to the whole ocean every 8 million years.

We had no idea of such turnover before. There was nothing beyond the rivers and the sediments. Now, we think the chemical transformations are very, very large, so that the total amount of material transported (out through these seafloor vents) is as large or larger than the amount brought in by the rivers.

So the salts in the sea are as much controlled by this geothermal activity as they are by the rivers. And this means that the way we look at the oceans through geologic time has completely changed.

As for the ores, Edmond explained that the flow of hot water through the underground fissures and up through the ore-rich chimneys "provides a mechanism for transporting these things (the metals) to places where they can precipitate" and form valuable ore bodies. It was found, for example, that the black smokers are rich in mineral species that are being changed by quick contact with the cold, alkaline seawater. "The water is clear" when seen down inside the vent, Edmond said, but "on mixing with the seawater, everything precipitates as a sulfide ore."

Ores of this type, rich in various metals, have been found in commercially valuable deposits, such as those on the island of Cyprus. Indeed, strange deposits seen on Cyprus—which scientists had been unable to explain—are now seen to be these weird, exotic chimneys that have fallen over, becoming part of the ore body.

"Nobody before," Edmond said, "has ever seen these deposits in the process of formation. There hasn't been any clear understanding of how these things formed. Now this tells us an awful lot about how they were formed, and perhaps how to explore for them."

The mineral deposits being formed off Mexico, however, are probably in water that is too deep—8,900 feet (2,800 meters)—to be commercially useful, but the deposits on Cyprus, formed some 2 billion years ago, do show that such deposits have good potential for exploitation.

This deep undersea work has also shown that there can be various types of underground pressure cookers, which are referred to by Edmond and colleagues as "tight systems" and "leaky systems." In the tight systems, the ultrahot water—laden with metallic elements—is forced to the surface rapidly, not mixing with other water until it comes gushing out of the seafloor chimney. At that point, on contact with cold seawater, the minerals precipitate out quickly.

In leaky systems, the water flowing underground mixes with other cooler, less acidic water. When that happens, some of the dissolved minerals are lost, probably coming out to form other types of deposits at great depth, but not forming the tall chimneys from which the water plume spews.

Thus the 21 Degrees North site is an example of a tight system in operation, forming black smokers and the metal-rich chimneys that act rather like fire hoses. The white smokers are thought to be merely "black smokers that have leaks in them."

It is because of such discoveries that, in Edmond's opinion, this has become "the most exciting work going on in the earth sciences today."

5 | *The Cascade Family of Volcanoes*

Before Mount St. Helens began its massive eruption of 1980, among the things climbers enjoyed most on reaching the top were spectacular views to the north, east, and south. Off in the distance, one could see Mount Rainier, Mount Adams, and Mount Hood poking their craggy, snowy crests up through the Pacific Northwest's characteristic blanket of clouds and mist. From that vantage point it becomes obvious that the Pacific Northwest is a land of volcanoes. Indeed, if one could see far enough north and south, a whole family of tall volcanic peaks would be seen dominating the terrain from northern California on up past the Canadian border.

And, like Mount St. Helens, these other mountains in western Canada, Washington, Oregon, and northern California have all gone through their own histories of fire and violence, each created through release of tremendous energy forcing its way up through the earth's fractured crust to burst through the surface. The members of this chain of large, relatively young volcanoes include Mount Garibaldi in British Columbia, Canada, Mount Baker and Glacier Peak north and east of Seattle, tall Mount Rainier slightly south and east of Seattle; Mount Adams, Mount St. Helens, Mount Hood, Mount Jefferson, the Three Sisters, Mount Thielsen, Crater Lake (Mount Mazama), Mount McLoughlin, Mount Shasta and Lassen Peak.

In addition, however, in between, adjacent to, or even far from these volcanoes are numerous other cinder cones, craters, fumaroles and lava flows that mark volcanic activity in the Pacific Northwest. Thus the Cascade volcanoes are not the only signs of volcanism in that region, merely the most immediately spectacular.

As should have been expected, of course, once Mount St. Helens erupted, attention was focused quickly, closely, on these other members of the Cascade Range's volcanic family. It became important to ask, Which volcano might go next?

As it turned out, it did not take long to receive at least a partial answer. Only 49 days after Mount St. Helens blew away one whole side of its peak, awakening everyone to the awesome possibilities of volcanism, seismologists got the first hints that something was going on beneath nearby Mount Hood. Beginning on July 6, 1980, a series of more than 50 earthquakes—some of them definitely located under the 11,235-foot- (3,424-meter-) tall mountain—were recorded, with a few others occasionally recorded near erupting Mount St. Helens.

Earth scientists were unable to say precisely what was occurring beneath Mount Hood, but their nervousness was evident as they looked at Mount St. Helens's violent activity and the possibility of a repeat performance from Mount Hood. Like Mount St. Helens, Mount Hood is also about 50 miles (80 kilometers) from Portland, Oregon, but to the southeast.

The seismic activity beneath Mount Hood began that Sunday evening at 6:17 P.M. with a shallow temblor registering 3.3 on the Richter scale of magnitude. This first tremor was followed only minutes later by a series of smaller earthquakes located about 10 miles (16 kilometers) southeast of Mount St. Helens.

Aftershocks from both regions were then recorded until about midnight, breaking loose at 2- or 3-minute intervals. These finally subsided, but about 7 A.M. the next day, another magnitude 3 temblor was recorded near Mount Hood. In the next few days a few more quakes of similar size were recorded at both Mount St. Helens and Mount Hood.

The US Geological Survey emphasized that "no immediate conclusions should be drawn about the possibilities of an eruption of Mount Hood because of earthquake activity." But the agency's scientists did add that "if the earthquakes are indeed centered beneath the mountain, then it could reflect movement of magma into a conduit of the mountain." At the time, however, such speculation was considered premature.

The concern about a possible eruption of Mount Hood, to go along with the activity on Mount St. Helens, was certainly warranted. Mount Hood, like the rest of the Cascade volcanoes, has a history of fitful eruptive activity. At the summit, climbers have reported seeing active fumaroles that continually emit steam. The last minor eruption of Mount Hood was recorded in 1865, but its last major eruption—an event probably marked by emission of steam and ash plus mudslides—was probably from 200 to 300 years ago.

Mount Hood stands as the centerpiece in scenic Mount Hood National Forest. The peak has been extensively eroded by glacial action, and a number of small glaciers have been mapped on the mountain. The peak's lower slopes are densely forested, mainly with conifers, and these areas provide a popular, important winter sports zone.

Along with Mount St. Helens and Mount Hood, then, this long string of very tall volcanoes—called stratovolcanos because of their steep-sloped flanks—stands as the most obvious sign of the violent geothermal activity that has gradually constructed the present version of the Pacific Northwest. Along with much other evidence farther inland, this family of volcanoes testifies that the United States, and especially the western United States, has been one of the most violently active volcanic regions in the world.

This history of violent volcanic activity quickly becomes evident to people traveling east from the Cascade Range. In western Washington and Oregon and on into Idaho, for example, vast areas can be seen where massive sheets of very liquid basalt—called flood lava—flowed rapidly over the landscape long ago. These massive, apparently fast-moving flows came boiling and streaming from long fissures, and they spread out over an area of 200,000 square miles (518,000 square kilometers) to form large plateaus, such as the Columbia River Plateau of Washington and Oregon, and the Snake River Plains of Idaho. Geologists have found evidence that lava flow after lava flow piled up over the years to form these large geological features, which in some places are 1,000 feet (300 meters) thick. The Columbia Plateau's total volume of basaltic lava, indeed, comes close to 100,000 cubic miles (400,000 cubic kilometers).

This lava, erupting from fissures, was apparently incredibly fluid, almost as fluid as water, since individual flows have been traced for distances of more than 100 miles (160 kilometers) and have covered so much territory so uniformly. Thus the name flood lavas.

In these areas, and especially in the rugged zone known as the Craters of the Moon National Monument on the northern edge of the Snake River Plains, the two types of lavas known as *aa* and *pahoehoe* are found. These words—aa and pahoehoe—are the

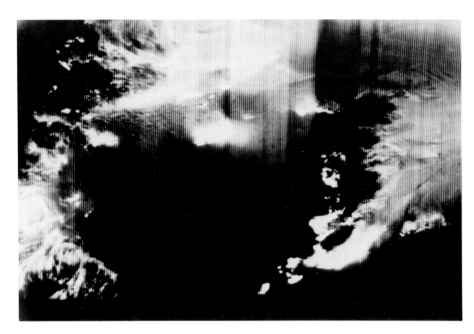

An active fumarole at Crater Rock on Mount Hood stands out as a bright thermal anomaly—flanked by heated ground—in this thermograph. (Oregon Army National Guard image)

Hawaiian terms that have been adopted worldwide for the two main types of basaltic lavas. Pahoehoe is a very fluid lava that takes on a smooth to ropey surface texture. Its flows tend to travel relatively long distances. Aa, a more viscous lava, forms steep-sided flows that seem to be composed largely of chunky blocks of rock that creep along apparently by falling over each other. Inside the flow, however, there is a continuous fluid interior.

In some cases, the surface and sides of such lava flows can solidify while the interior is still quite liquid and flowing. Eventually, the lava can drain out of the interior, leaving a tubular crust that forms long tunnels, or lava tubes. It has been found, too, that sometimes water can enter these tubes and freeze in winter. And, because the tube's walls are such good insulating material, the ice in the tubes may remain frozen all summer, even in desert areas. Excellent examples of such lava tubes and ice caves can be seen in the Modoc Lava Beds National Monument in California.

This volcanic activity is not necessarily very old. On the northern edge of the Snake River Plains, at the Craters of the Moon National Monument, for instance, the basaltic lavas are thought to have erupted only 2,000 years ago. Along the Snake River in Idaho, these massive flows are beautifully exposed, and in some areas they measure more than a mile thick. The volcanic vents found in the region today are located along gigantic fissures, and the vents now range in construction from cinder cones that are built entirely of red and black frothy lava cinders to what are called spatter cones, which were formed by liquid lava blobs piling up around the vent.

Such evidence testifies vividly that at some time over the past 70 million years, volcanic rocks covered nearly all of the western states—Washington, Oregon, California, Nevada, Arizona, Utah, Idaho, and substantial portions of Montana, Colorado, Wyoming, Texas, and New Mexico.

At present, however, active volcanism in the United States is limited to the Aleutian Islands, Alaska, Hawaii, and the Cascade Mountains of the Pacific Northwest. The Hawaiian Islands themselves are made up almost completely of volcanic rocks that were erupted from some of the most active, largest volcanoes in the world, so-called shield volcanoes. One of these volcanoes, in fact, rises almost 30,000 feet (9,000 meters) from the seafloor. Shield volcanoes are so named because they build very large, broad cones that only gradually slope upward toward the peak. They take this broader shape because the lavas are typically less viscous, usually flowing rather far from the vent before solidifying.

Best known among the Hawaiian volcanoes, of course, is Mauna Loa, the world's largest volcano. It shares the island of Hawaii with the world's most active volcano, Kilauea, which in an eruption in 1959–1960 was seen spewing a fountain of glowing lava 1,900 feet (600 meters) into the air. Kilauea, in fact, is of special interest, since its lava comes from very deep inside the earth, giving geologists a sort of window into the globe's interior.

Also of great interest to geologists are the Aleutian volcanoes, which occupy the 2,000-mile- (3,200-kilometer-) long Aleutian Island Arc. This system includes 36 volcanoes that have been active within recorded history, plus many more extinct volcanoes. Examples of the active cones are those named Pavlof, Shishaldin, and Pavlof Sister. There is also a "disappearing volcano" on Bogoslof Island, since it has emerged from the sea and then submerged more than once in recorded history.

Alaska, too, has its share of active volcanoes. One of the most remarkable is Mount Katmai on the Alaska Peninsula. From the base of this volcano, in 1912, an estimated two cubic miles of ash and pumice erupted in the form of incandescent avalanches. Early explorers called this phenomenon the River of Sand, and it flowed more than 15 miles (24 kilometers) down a large glacial valley, filling it to a depth of more than 400 feet (120 meters). This valley then became known as the Valley of Ten Thousand Smokes because of the thousands of steaming fumaroles that pushed steam and acrid fumes through the surface. These fumaroles continued venting steam and gas for many years after the eruption.

In the Cascade Mountains, however, in contrast to the massive, very liquid flows of lava to the east, the volcanoes have built what are called composite cones. This means these high Cascade volcanoes were constructed primarily of lavas called andesites, which are intermediate in chemical composition between the lavas called basalts and rhyolites. These andesitic volcanoes usually produce tall cones of rubble that consist of layer upon layer of lava flows, ash deposits, and mudflows.

During an eruption, volcanic mudflows can either be hot or cold and are capable of shoving around boulders that weigh many tons, depositing them in rather unlikely places. This type of mudflow—called a lahar—is commonly found on the flanks of Cascade volcanoes such as Mount Rainier.

Before Mount St. Helens erupted in the spring of 1980, perhaps the most famous of the Cascade volcanoes was Mount Mazama, which is more widely known as beautifully scenic Crater Lake. This huge volcanic cone is what is called a caldera, since all that is left of a once majestic mountain peak are the lower flanks and a deep hole in the ground. Nonetheless, the remaining rim of this volcanic structure still reaches an altitude of 8,160 feet (2,486 meters) in some places. In the hole, of course, is beautiful, deep blue Crater Lake.

From what earth scientists have been able to make of the geologic evidence, no event in the long volcanic history of Oregon was more dramatic than the decapitation of the mountain called Mazama. In fact, the 14,000-foot- (4,300-meter-) tall mountain blew its own head off, and enormous amounts of volcanic ash and dust were erupted, most of it being tossed high into the sky, with the rest boiling down the slopes as devastating avalanches. Geologists who have studied the mountain, including geochemist Willard F. Libby, used radioactive carbon dating techniques to calculate that this eruption occurred some 6,600 years ago. In all, research indicates that a huge volume of volcanic ash erupted out of the massive lava chamber within a short time. This sudden ejection of material rapidly depleted the supply of lava in the magma chamber beneath the volcano, seriously weakening the upper structure and leaving it without support. As a result, the remainder of the mountain apparently collapsed into the vacated chamber, forming the large depression that was later filled with water to become Crater Lake. Today the basin measures 4 to 6 miles (6.5 to 9.5 kilometers) across and is some 4,000 feet (1,200 meters) deep.

Above:
Spectacular panoramic photo shows Crater Lake in the collapsed summit caldera of Oregon's Mount Mazama. (Oregon Army National Guard photo)

Right:
View of Mount Lassen in northern California shows area that was devastated along the northeast flank—to the right of the peak—during the lateral blast that accompanied the eruption of May 22, 1915. (Oregon Army National Guard photo)

Eventually, a last series of smaller eruptions produced a number of smaller cinder cones inside the caldera, one of which is Wizard Island, which is visible in the lake.

Geologists who have studied the remains of Mount Mazama have estimated, indeed, that Mount Mazama shot about 42 cubic kilometers of ash and dust into the sky, thoroughly dwarfing the 1980 performance of Mount St. Helens—only 1 cubic kilometer. The lake occupying Mount Mazama's collapse crater, or caldera, has been measured at 1,720 feet (525 meters) deep, which makes it the deepest lake in North America.

Perhaps the next most famous of the Cascade volcanoes is Mount Lassen, or Lassen Peak, in northern California. Mount Lassen is the southernmost peak in the Cascade chain and, until Mount St. Helens erupted, had been the most recently active, in terms of a true large eruption. The reawakening of the big Mount Lassen volcano began in 1914 and continued for about a seven-year period. Observers at the time reported that the eruption apparently began suddenly, without any precursor earthquakes or obvious warming. Of course, modern monitoring techniques would probably have recorded some sort of precursory activity if the new instruments had been available.

This 10,000-foot- (3,000-meter-) tall peak, located east of the California town of Red Bluff, is too far south, compared to the other Cascade volcanoes, to maintain large glaciers, or even to remain snow covered throughout the summer. As a result, tourists driving north or south on the relatively new Interstate Highway 5 see Mount Lassen as a barren, earth-toned dome on the eastern horizon. On closer inspection, however, the Lassen dome can be seen displaying its tinted rocks in shades of slatey blue, pinks, and grays.

The first official recording of activity from Mount Lassen came on May 30, 1914, when a local resident, Bert McKenzie, who was looking at the peak directly, reported that shortly before 5 P.M. the mountain suddenly spit up a dense black cloud of ash that he referred to as smoke. This first blast was estimated to have shot several hundred feet into the air.

In a close investigation of what was going on, Forest Ranger Harvey Abbey worked his way up through the deep snow to reach the summit on Sunday, May 31, where he found a fresh new crater measuring 100 feet (30 meters) long by 30 feet (8 meters) wide on the northwestern wall of the peak's old summit crater. Larger explosive eruptions occurred in the following days, some of them hurling large boulders outward onto the mountain's flanks.

On the following June 15, a party of hikers climbed Lassen for a look at the new crater. They were close by when an eruption occurred, and described themselves as lucky to have escaped alive. Subsequent eruptions were even larger, however, hurling ash and rock fragments as high as 9,200 feet (2,800 meters) into the air, and a month later another even bigger eruption tossed ash and debris still higher.

Then the pattern of activity changed. On August 22, for example, instead of firing its cloud of gas and ash straight up, the cloud was expelled at an oblique angle and then came cascading down the mountainside. It was an early warning of what would become the mountain's most dangerous form of activity, lateral blasts similar to, but smaller than, the massive directed blast that erupted from Mount St. Helens on May 18, 1980.

Eruptions, mostly uncounted because of the sparse population and the cloudy weather in the area, continued through the first of the year and into the next spring, when the climax of this first eruptive period occurred, marked by the first sighting of lava emerging from the crater. The flow of lava soon unleashed a large mudflow on the northeastern side of the peak that went pouring down into Lost Creek, then topped a divide and dumped itself into Hat Creek. As it moved, carrying blocks of hot lava weighing as much as 20 tons, the mudflow overwhelmed everything in its path, including trees, bridges, buildings, and fences, burying once fertile fields.

But this was just the beginning. The erupting mountain was building up pressure for even more violent activity, and it reached the breaking point on the afternoon of May 22, 1915. As thousands of northern California's settlers watched, the mountain belched out a huge black cloud of hot ash that rose to a height of perhaps 6 miles (10 kilometers) and then began raining ash on the northern Sacramento Valley. And as this huge plume moved upward and to the east, at the same time a horizontal blast was hurrying downward across the mountain's northeast slope, again into valleys known as Hat Creek and Lost Creek. And, like what occurred in the blast from Mount St. Helens in 1980, this hot hurricanelike flow of gas and debris rushed through the thick stands of timber, snapping 6-foot- (2-meter-) diameter tree trunks as if they were matchsticks. Again, another mudflow was unleashed from the peak to go grinding its way through these two heavily punished valleys.

From this point on, however, activity began tapering off, punctuated occasionally by brief eruptions that still sent large dark clouds of ash streaming into the sky. The last reports of activity came in 1921, and that action was listed merely as large clouds of steam being released from the eastern side of the mountain.

Technical Vignette: Thermal infrared images
Charles Rosenfeld

Catastrophic volcanic eruptions have occurred within historical times at several volcanoes that were considered extinct. Since there had been no visible activity in advance of such eruptions, people living nearby did not have time to prepare, and many died as a result. Among such events the best known were the eruptions of Vesuvius in 79 A.D. (which wiped out Pompeii), Lammington in New Guinea in 1951, and the 1968 eruption of Arenal in Costa Rica. Precursory changes—such as earth tremors, swelling of the volcano's cone, tilting of the ground surface, changes in gas emission, and thermal anomalies such as changes in fumaroles or increases in water temperatures in hotsprings and crater lakes—which might be detectable with proper instruments, almost certainly occurred. But nobody was watching, and obviously many of the instruments for monitoring such changes did not then exist.

With modern instrumentation, however, that situation is changing. Microminiaturization of components has made it possible to employ useful precision instruments in critical areas and monitor their readings from afar. In addition, remote-sensing instruments have been developed that allow near-constant surveillance of dangerous areas from safe distances. Among such instruments are infrared sensors, which are capable of detecting and imaging heat flow patterns as heat is being radiated from volcanoes. Such instruments have been mounted aboard aircraft and have been used for observations of volcanoes in Hawaii,

Italy, Iceland, Mount St. Helens, and in over 20 other volcanic regions.

Unfortunately, however, the results from thermal infrared (IR) imaging have been rather mixed, something less than spectacular. As R. M. Moxham has pointed out, "Results to date are more tantalizing than elucidating. At some volcanoes, thermal forerunners (of eruptions) have been well documented; elsewhere, temperature measurements have been inconclusive or negative."

Most thermal IR surveys reported in the literature consisted of a single flight, or at best several flights spread over a few months' time. Many such surveys employed either experimental or antiquated IR scanners, and few were ever verified by ground surveys; deficiencies in equipment or coverage may be partly to blame, therefore, for poor results.

Thermal scanning of volcanoes in the Cascade Range began with systematic coverage of Washington's Mount Rainier and several other prominent volcanic peaks, as sponsored by the US Geological Survey in 1964, 1966, and 1969. IR coverage was then extended to virtually every other peak in the range; in addition, some ground verification of the results was made.

The big thrust in thermal IR imaging began, however, when the Sherman crater atop Mount Baker, in northern Washington, began heating up in 1975. In that year the Oregon Army National Guard made numerous survey flights over the hot ground and the fu-

maroles in the crater, and then began to acquire systematic IR imagery over the rest of the Cascade volcanoes. This effort has continued under the title of the Cascade Surveillance Project, and the Mohawk aerial surveillance planes have repeatedly taken images of the shifting heat patterns detected on some of the prominent peaks.

Among these Cascade volcanoes, Mount St. Helens had perhaps the most consistent thermal anomalies among those imaged over several years. The crater fumaroles atop Mount Rainier have occasionally shifted location; Mount Hood and Mount Lassen have undergone brief "hot flashes"; but the small steam vent beneath the talus deposit on Mount St. Helens's southwest flank has remained essentially unchanged.

But in 1980 the activity at Mount St. Helens began picking up. On March 27, after nearly a week of seismic activity beneath the peak, a National Guard Mohawk plane—piloted by Portland State University's wrestling coach, Len Kaufman—spotted a small round perforation in the ice shrouding Mount St. Helens's summit. A thin streak of gray ash could be seen on the snow, trailing off toward the southeast. Shortly after noon, a sharp sound like an explosion was heard in the Portland, Oregon, area. Many people dismissed the noise as merely a sonic boom from an airplane, but for geologists—who had been tipped off by the seismic activity—it was the signal for which they had been waiting. Indeed, the explosion was the first phreatic eruption, a steam blast, on the cloud-shrouded summit.

And by 2:40 P.M. the Guard's Mohawk aircraft had photographed the new 70-meter-diameter explosion crater, and thermal IR line scanners had detected at least three separate clusters of active fumaroles.

After a second explosion crater began forming on March 29, the Oregon National Guard began routine nighttime scanning runs from east to west over the summit, at altitudes only 450 meters above the crater rim. These night runs were essential in order to detect the heat emitted from the crater area without interference by reflected solar heat. These night images showed that even after the two explosion craters joined, separate thermal anomalies remained, and they were connected by a line of smaller hot spots aligned along a fault bounding the south rim of the crater.

By April 15 the overflights had detected a series of hot spots on the northeast flank of Mount St. Helens. These were forming a conspicuous alignment through the expanding bulge area of the Forsyth Glacier. The continued expansion of the bulge, and the cessation of phreatic explosions within the crater, prompted a ground-verification expedition into the crater. For this we used an Oregon National Guard UH-1 helicopter equipped with a thermal IR radiometer, an electronic device that calculates radiant temperature by measuring the wavelengths of the electromagnetic energy emitted by an object, making it possible to take the temperature of a hot

object without actually touching it. The helicopter also enabled us to hover close by, allowing small areas within the crater to be examined. Also, the rotor wash (wind from the rotor) was used to blow away the steam plumes that tend to mask the fumaroles and prevent accurate readings.

These readings with the radiometer, when coupled with the thermal IR scanning image taken the previous night, provided the basis for making a computer map showing temperatures by color. The Mohawk aircraft's crew was also enabled to obtain almost instantaneous thermal IR images in flight; these were later converted into color-coded temperature maps.

Another system, a more technologically advanced instrument used by the US Geological Survey, is able to record the thermal IR scanner data on magnetic tape. The recorded information is then processed digitally by computer and can be used to build a similar color-coded thermal map. Also, by incorporating a calibration reference within the scanner, no ground verification is necessary. Despite its superior ability to resolve temperature differences, however, it provides no real-time image for immediate interpretation.

It was this difference in operational characteristics between systems that led to confusion among news people concerning the last surveillance flights run just prior to the big eruption of May 18. Although a decision was made not to process the US Geological Survey's magnetic tape data taken Friday, May 16, until the next Monday, this did not change the acquisition of real-time thermal IR images by the National Guard planes on the evening of May 17 and the morning of May 18.

And, since the national Guard's May 17–18 images showed that the heat patterns that had been developing since April 15 were essentially unchanged, there was no obvious cause for alarm. The only apparently significant change that might have been seen was the increased size of a thermal anomaly located at the base of the bulge area. The instability of the bulge, of course, was already well known, since a 50,000-cubic-meter avalanche of rock had come cascading down from that area on May 12.

The last IR image—taken less than 3 hours before the explosive eruption—still showed the pair of remarkably persistent heat anomalies associated with the two early explosion craters. In addition, the image confirmed the instability of the bulge area and pinpointed the locations of various hot spots surrounding the elliptical mass of the bulge. But it must still be emphasized that nothing seen in this remarkable image indicates convincingly that the mountain was rapidly building toward a cataclysmic eruption.

During that eruption, however, direct flights over the crater were impossible because of the dense and turbulent ash plume. But flights over the pyroclastic debris that flowed down the Toutle River valley were made on May 19. The images taken then and others taken following each of the subsequent major eruptions illustrate the structure and perhaps the dynamics of these hot flows. Although these flows look like jumbled rock piles to most observers, the thermal IR images reveal heat patterns within them that resemble the mixing of viscous fluids, such as oil paints. The lobes and swirls detected not only establish the chronology of deposition for geological study, but may be of value for the study of fluid dynamics as well.

Once the clouds associated with the eruption (which attenuate thermal IR signals) had dissipated, this form of imagery again proved valuable for assessing the growth of the several lava domes that formed in the crater. High-temperature sensors were used to detect inflation of the dacite lava masses as the bread-crust surfaces crackled during swelling periods. And with the appearance of multiple-dome complexes in the period from December 1980 to February 1981, the thermal IR images were of special value, for they showed stresses developing as fractures were radiating from the domes, as well as the heat being emitted from the inflating portions of the dome complex.

The eruption of Mount St. Helens has been the occasion for demonstrating, among other things, the value of the systematic application of thermal IR image taking to the study of volcanic phenomena.

The arrow points out the crater area and the line of hot spots that descends down the Mount St. Helens northwest flank and across the bulge area. (Oregon National Guard image, Oregon State University enhancement)

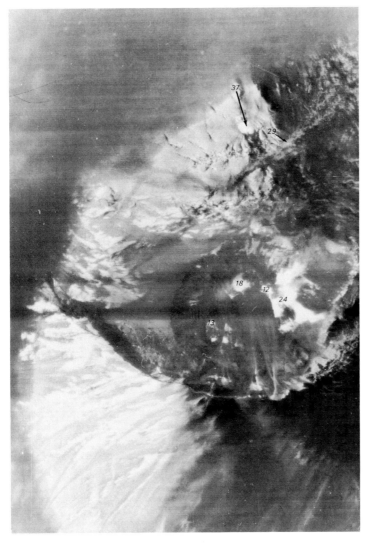

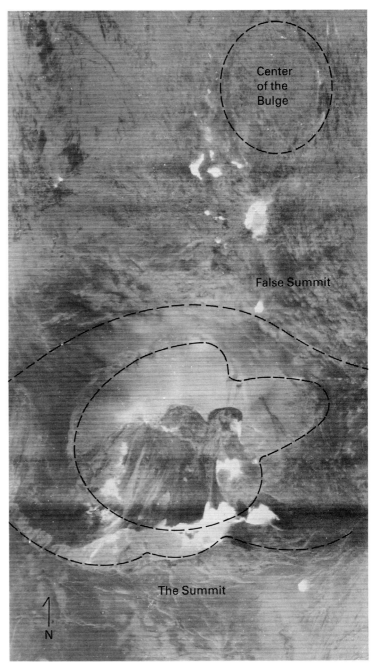

Above:
Thermograph image that was later verified by a helicopter survey flight on April 30, 1980.

Right:
Detailed image of the crater and bulge area, from a thermograph acquired by an Oregon Army National Guard Mohawk aircraft, 5:52 A.M., May 18, 1980.

Above:
Image of heat patterns on the surface of the pyroclastic flows that
descended into the Toutle River
valley during the eruption of July
22, 1980.

Right:
Thermograph showing the dome
complex in the crater on January
19, 1981. The image shows radial
fractures, a thrust fault, and at least
four distinct areas of dome
formation.

Mount Lassen is famous among volcanoes because the main vent has built up one of the largest known volcanic plug domes. Such a dome is formed when very viscous, pasty lava is pushed up vertically. It can remain standing even above the rim of the crater, and may in some instances be completely blown away by subsequent eruptions. Indeed, the large Goat Rocks dome on Mount St. Helens was completely shattered, disappearing in the huge eruption of 1980. The mechanism by which such domes are built may be compared to the way gooey toothpaste squeezed from its tube retains the shape of the tube's neck.

Such domes can form into steep-sided—even vertical—rather craggy knobs or *spines*, while others may form relatively short, steep-sided lava structures known as *coulées*.

It is known, too, that eruptions from beneath such domes can be among the most dangerous. The gases dissolved in the buried magma can suddenly burst forth with great violence—as seen at Mount St. Helens—and cause the formation of the extremely mobile, sometimes incandescent avalanches of hot rock, dust, steam, and gas. In extreme cases, these avalanches can travel as fast as 100 miles (160 kilometers) an hour, burning their way down the volcano's slopes and devastating everything in their path.

Indeed, it was an eruption of just this type that shattered Mount Pelée in Martinique, the West Indies, in 1902, killing as many as 30,000 people. In the town of St. Pierre, the only lucky survivor was a man who had been locked away in St. Pierre's dismal, poorly ventilated jail. This eruption of Mount Pelée was so spectacular, indeed, that similar eruptions have since been referred to as Peléan eruptions or explosions.

Another Cascade volcano that has caused recent worry, especially for the people living north of Seattle, Washington, is 10,800-foot- (3,285-meter-) tall Mount Baker, located some 110 miles (175 kilometers) to the north of the city and 15 miles (24 kilometers) south of the Canadian border. In 1975 Mount Baker began showing signs of activity, venting large amounts of steam from its summit crater. At the time, the main concern was that the melting ice on the peak's glaciers would produce huge mud-slides that could come bounding down the steep slopes, filling lakes, destroying hydroelectric power stations and ruining reservoirs and recreational facilities.

Mount Baker—before Mount St. Helens erupted in 1980—was known to have the most thermally active summit crater among the Cascade volcanoes. This activity increased rather dramatically on March 10, 1975, when the Sherman crater—which is distinct from the older, snow-filled summit crater—suddenly increased activity in its fumaroles. An unusually large dark gray plume was seen rising above the crater's rim. Soon thereafter, aerial photos showed interesting changes in the crater, including rather large new steam vents, melt pits, new crevasses, and ponds of meltwater. A very thin veil of dust, too, was seen decorating the snowpack around the crater.

As spring and summer wore on, fumarole activity accelerated, and the glacial ice kept melting until, in August, some snow-free ground appeared near the crater, revealing the presence of more fumaroles than had been anticipated.

Unlike what happened at Mount St. Helens in 1980, however, Mount Baker remained essentially seismically quiet, even though heating was obvious. Even in 1980, for example, 30,000 square yards (24,000 square meters) of hot ground remained snow free around the crater on Mount Baker.

The previously known significant activity on Mount Baker was in 1843, when the ejecta that spewed out consisted mainly of ash. Even so, there appeared to be very little material deposited on the cone or on the surroundings during this episode. The peak itself is composed largely of andesitic lava.

As the northernmost of the American Cascade volcanoes, Mount Baker receives a very heavy annual snowfall, and because of this it supports some 20 square miles (52 square kilometers) of active glaciers. One danger in a major eruption, of course, is that such a large load of ice may be rather quickly melted, increasing the hazards from flooding and mudslides—so much so, indeed, that a proposed site for a nuclear power plant, in the Skagit River valley below the mountain, was in doubt for safety reasons.

Left:
During a spurt of activity in April 1975, ash is shown staining the surface of the Boulder Glacier that surrounds the Sherman Crater atop Mount Baker, in northern Washington.

Below:
Glacial ice began melting rapidly, breaking up into large blocks and collapsing into the Sherman Crater on Mount Baker, September 1975.

Studies of the eruptive history of Mount Baker indicate that during the past 10,000 years airborne pyroclastic materials have been erupted from the peak at least four times. There have also been at least two lava flows, numerous mudflows, and at least one pyroclastic avalanche. The most recent major ashfall, found on the eastern side of the peak, was estimated—through radioactive dating techniques—to have occurred some 400 years ago.

Glacier Peak stands some 60 miles (100 kilometers) to the south and slightly to the east of Mount Baker and is 95 miles (150 kilometers) northeast of Seattle. This volcano has been asleep for perhaps 12,000 years, and has shown no recent signs of reawakening. Its 10,500-foot- (3,213-meter-) tall cone is made up mostly of dacite lava, similar to that extruded from the throat of Mount St. Helens in 1980 and 1981.

Like Mount Baker, Glacier Peak is heavily laden with snowfields and large glaciers that have been carving away at its flanks for thousands of years. Geologists noted, indeed, that the original volcanic surfaces of the peak have been radically altered by glacial action. The Chocolate and Scimitar glaciers, for example, flow, respectively, from the summit crater's breached eastern and western walls. On the north wall can be seen traces of yellow stains, which suggest that the rocks may have been altered by acidic fumes and steam coming from fumaroles within the crater or close by.

This peak, while only 350 feet (100 meters) lower than Mount Baker, is not well known, even to the people who live in the Pacific Northwest. Access to the mountain is difficult, since no roads allow close approach, and it is shielded behind a series of deep valleys, steep cliffs, and icy barriers.

Even though Glacier Peak has been utterly quiet now for some 12,000 years, geologists believe that in its last eruption the volcano produced one of the most violently explosive events in the history of the Cascade Range. In that siege of activity, the mountain produced enormous amounts of light gray pumice that was caught by winds and carried for hundreds of miles to the east. Geologists report evidence for at least nine large eruptions, apparently within a relatively short period of time. Even after 12,000 years of weathering, there remains a deep layer of gray pumice some 4 meters thick stretching as far as 12 miles (19 kilometers) downwind.

As with the Mount St. Helens eruption of 1980, ash deposits were spread over most of eastern Washington State and into Idaho, Montana, and Canada. The volume of ash produced by this series of eruptions thus approaches the volume of ash produced by the incredibly violent eruption of Mount Mazama some 6,000 years later. These two spectacular ashfalls have given geologists a relatively accurate clock for timing the volcanic events that have occurred in the Pacific Northwest. Unlike Mount Mazama, however, and despite the huge volume of ash ejected from the cone, Glacier Peak did not collapse in upon itself. Instead, the mountain produced another explosive eruption from the summit crater, this time sending a broiling avalanche of hot gases, steam, rocks, and ash hurrying down the mountain's western slope. This flow covered the previous material, including the blanket of pumice, beneath a blanket of glassy fragments of debris that extended for miles down the valleys and ravines.

Among geologists, Glacier Peak is remarkable now for its 12,000-year-old layer of pumiceous ash that overlays a cone built mainly of dacitic lava. Indeed, the main features high on the volcanic cone are several dacite domes, including two on the south and east slopes. The dome on the south flank is called Disappointment Peak, and it forms a rounded knot on the relatively smooth slope.

The second large dacite dome, on the east flank of the volcano, is some 2,200 feet (750 meters) below the mountain's summit. This dome, which oozed from a vent high on the mountain's side, contains dacitic lava that was unusually viscous and brittle, since it broke apart rapidly, creating avalanches and mudflows that cascaded down into the Suiattle River valley. This activity radically changed the flow pattern of the river and drainage on the eastern side of Glacier Peak, having overwhelmed the valley, forcing the river into a new course against the bedrock slopes to the east.

Perhaps the most spectacular of the Cascade volcanoes is Mount Rainier, the 14,400-foot- (4,392-meter-) tall peak located only 46 miles (75 kilometers) southeast of Seattle. Even though this volcano almost constantly emits steam from numerous fumaroles, it has been essentially dormant for more than 2,000 years. It has been speculated, however, that Mount Rainier might have erupted only 500 years ago, before records were kept. Mount Rainier, too, is an andesitic volcano.

Like Mount Baker and Glacier Peak, Mount Rainier is being carved and chiseled by the large glaciers that occupy its flanks. Mount Rainier, however, now supports the largest single system of glaciers among the Cascade volcanoes and, indeed, within the contiguous United States. There are 26 named glaciers decorating its flanks, and the meltwater from these are the sources of important rivers: the White, Nisqually, Puyallup, Cowlitz, and Carbon rivers.

Because of its size, its glaciers, and its obviously violent volcanic history, Mount Rainier has been a favorite for geologic study, and this work has shown clearly that the volcano was once much larger and much higher than it is today. There is also ample evidence that Mount Rainier is merely slumbering and cannot be considered at all extinct. Within the past 10,000 years, for example, this volcano has produced at least 55 large mudflows, several broiling hot avalanches of rocky debris, at least one period involving flows of lava and 12 eruptions of volcanic ash. One of the most spectacular mudflows came down the mountain some 6,000 years ago, delivering 610 million cubic meters of debris down the White River for a distance of 30 miles (50 kilometers).

But spectacular as that was, it cannot compare to what happened about 1,000 years later, or 5,000 years ago, when in a massive, cataclysmic eruption the Osceola mudflow was created, letting loose some 2 billion cubic meters of muddy debris that flowed down the mountain to cover some 115 square miles (325 square kilometers) of flatland close to Puget Sound. In the latter event, the wave of debris—which is thought to have pushed across valley floors at speeds close to 40 miles (65 kilometers) an hour— was triggered by collapse of Mount Rainier's former summit, which fell apart as if shaken into dust. Geologists believe that a rapid series of steam explosions pushed clouds of shattered rock and dust over the volcano's northeast side. At the same time, the summit itself slumped and toppled toward the east to form a speeding avalanche that must have been over 330 feet (100 meters) high.

One flow of debris rolled down the big Emmons Glacier while another found its way down the Winthrop Glacier and barged into the West Fork of the White River. When these flows finally met at the base of the mountain, they converged to flow another 60 miles (100 kilometers) across the Puget lowlands. Indeed, one lobe of this massive mudflow even reached an arm of Puget Sound, and in the process covered the areas where people now live in Kent, Auburn, Sumner, and Puyallup.

If such a mudflow were to be repeated, some 40,000 people living in the area west of the mountain, near Puget Sound, would find their lives and livelihoods endangered. The impact on the land, the economy, and human life would be massive and almost incalculable.

That huge eruption—like the eruption of Mount St. Helens in 1980—must have changed the appearance of Mount Rainier dramatically. Geologists estimate that this event created a bowl or caldera at the summit perhaps 2 miles (3 kilometers) in diameter that seemed tipped slightly toward the east. Indeed, the outlines of this huge double crater system can still be seen by the heat traces, the gas-emitting fumaroles that line the rim. Later eruptions have since contributed volcanic bombs, plus loads of pumice and lava flows, which began the process of rebuilding the shattered peak, leaving, in essence, a much younger mountain lodged atop the broken foundation of its predecessor. Indeed, within historic time there have been many small-scale eruptions, most occurring between 1820 and 1855, while the last event producing ash and steam was reported, perhaps too enthusiastically, in 1894.

Despite its relative quiescence, Mount Rainier is known, even now, to maintain areas where the rocks are hot and fumaroles are active. There are also places on its flanks that produce occasional steam explosions, and reports of such activity have been

View of Mount Rainier's southwest flank.

increasing. In the early 1960s, for example, mountain climbers reported being shaken by loud noises and the sight of a large column of steam pouring upward into the sky. In 1961, near Gibraltar Rock, a party reported seeing a hole blasted in the mountainside and a plume of steam spewing 150 feet (60 meters) into the sky. And in 1965, skiers reported steam issuing from a ridge near the Kautz Glacier.

Perhaps the largest such event in historical times was reported by forest rangers in 1963. They were some 12 miles (20 kilometers) northeast of the mountain when what appears to have been a steam explosion erupted. Once the clouds and snow cleared, the rangers—looking through field glasses—reported that a large amount of rock was covering the lower part of the Emmons Glacier. They were unable to see, however, that some 500 million cubic feet (14 million cubic meters) of rock debris—lavas and breccias—had broken from the north face of Little Tahoma Peak and had tumbled some 1,600 feet (500 meters), landing with terrific force on the glacier.

Later observers estimated that the rockfall, apparently afloat on a cushion of air, surged at perhaps 35 miles (60 kilometers) per hour over the end of the glacier, where it became airborne as it dashed down the canyon. In places, geologists reported, the rocky debris surged up the canyon walls some 330 feet (100 meters), and when it finally came to rest the debris was only about 1,650 feet (500 meters) from the White River Campground. In all, it had traveled 4 miles (6.5 kilometers), falling almost 6,500 feet (2,000 meters) down the mountain.

Since then various signs of activity—including sudden melting of ice near the summit, more steam explosions, and rock avalanches—have testified to the dangers buried within Mount Rainier. The evidence of activity was sufficiently strong that the US Geological Survey, in cooperation with scientists at the University of Washington, established a volcano watch at Mount Rainier. Among other things, this watch took infrared readings of heatflow at the summit, placed seismographs at several locations on the mountain, and installed heat-measuring devices inside the peak's west crater. This last instrument was designed to take the mountain's temperature daily, then relay the information

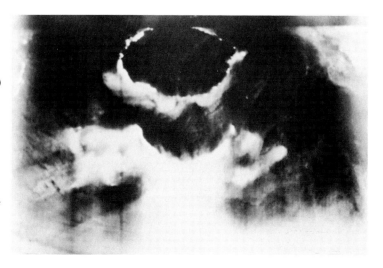

Infrared thermograph shows the fumaroles surrounding the summit crater on Mount Rainier.

to a satellite passing overhead in space. Unfortunately, the equipment in the crater survived only five weeks, a victim of the cold and wind.

Mount Adams, some 40 miles (65 kilometers) east of Mount St. Helens, is something of a mystery. Standing 13,200 feet (3,751 meters) tall, this strato-volcano is the second highest in the Cascade Range. It is made up largely of andesite, and is estimated to have been dormant some 3,000 or 4,000 years. There have been no recent signs of activity.

That Mount Adams is different is obvious. Rather than forming a beautifully symmetrical cone, such as was possessed by Mount St. Helens before 1980, Mount Adams seems almost squat, exhibiting an irregular summit lacking the striking grandeur of some of the other volcanoes, such as Rainier. Nonetheless, because of its size alone, Mount Adams makes an impression on visitors.

Geologists who have studied this mountain report that rather than being a single structure, Mount Adams appears to be more like three volcanic cones sort of propping each other up. The mountain's steep flanks have been deeply eroded by large glaciers. On the east side, for instance, the large Klickitat Glacier has slowly excavated a huge amphitheaterlike depression deep into the side of the mountain, creating the second-largest cirque of any of the active glaciers in the Cascades. (The largest is the Carbon Glacier, which is streaming slowly down Mount Rainier's northern flank.)

Actually, very little is known—or has been published—about the geology and the geological history of Mount Adams. Perhaps this is because the mountain is relatively remote, not really developed yet for recreation purposes, and is reachable only via logging roads and difficult climbing. Nonetheless, Mount Adams's summit crater has been the site of commercial mining activities—which began in the 1930s—because of the rich deposits of elemental sulfur found there. Also present are large deposits of gypsum and alum, in some places up to 30 feet (9 meters) thick.

Similar to Mount Baker and Mount Rainier, this mountain is made up primarily of andesitic lava flows interlaced with a few pyroclastic deposits. Mount Adams also has an unusually large number of smaller, parasitic volcanoes located around its flanks.

The only known action on this mountain has been a series of rather large rock flows, large avalanches, that have cascaded down the steep flanks. In 1921, for example, a large slide began on the mountain's west side, just 1,000 feet (300 meters) below the summit. In that one slide, an enormous amount of rock tumbled about a mile (1.6 kilometers)—in vertical distance—to cover some 6,000 acres (2,400 hectares) on the western slope. It was thought that this huge slide might have been touched off by a small steam explosion, similar to what was observed on Mount Rainier in 1963, although no recent signs of heat emission have been detected.

Given its low level of thermal activity, Mount Adams is considered a dormant volcano. Still, the emission of steam and sulfurous gases from crevices associated with the crater indicate heat still exists deep within the mountain, although these emissions seem to be growing weaker.

To the south of Mount Adams and Mount Hood stands Mount Jefferson, located directly east of Oregon's rich Willamette Valley. And like Mount Adams, Mount Jefferson is surrounded by a rather primitive, undeveloped wilderness area, which makes access to the peak very difficult.

Standing 10,300 feet (3,100 meters) high, Mount Jefferson is considered one of the most photogenic of the Cascade volcanoes. It has a very sharp, pointed summit that is dressed in abundant glacial ice. The peak was named by explorers on the Lewis and Clark expedition after the US president who sponsored their venture.

Mount Jefferson is the most deeply eroded of the Cascade volcanoes. The erosion has revealed that the volcano probably began as a pumice cone that was later encased in basaltic andesite, which in some places is as much as 2,200 feet (700 meters) thick. Lava flows have repeatedly coursed down its flanks to inundate nearby valleys.

Because very little study has been done on this mountain, little can be said about the dates of its most recent activity or its detailed history. The best estimate points to some cinder-cone activity about 6,500 years ago. In all, Mount Jefferson—despite its tall beauty—represents only a small amount of lava, especially when compared to the really productive volcanoes like Mount Mazama and Mount Rainier. Indeed, geologists suspect—based on evidence of little activity since the last glaciation and no steam or fumarole activity—that Mount Jefferson may even be extinct.

The Three Sisters volcanic region is a study in multiples. Not only are the three peaks of this structure spectacular as they stand shoulder to shoulder, but they are literally surrounded by other volcanic structures, such as Bachelor Butte, Broken Top, Le Conte Crater, Little Brother, Collier Cone, Yapoah Crater, Belknap Crater, Little Belknap, and Mount Washington. In other words, the Three Sisters—North Sister, Middle Sister, and South Sister—stand as the centerpiece in a region that has seen repeated and violently tumultuous volcanic activity.

Throughout the rest of the Cascade Range, of course, the major volcanoes tend to be spaced more than 40 miles (65 kilometers) apart. But here in central Oregon, this grouping of tall peaks—several of which are more than 10,000 feet (3,000 meters) tall—breaks the rules. And like nowhere else in the range, the evidence is strong for a great number and wide variety of eruptions, and the variety of glaciers chewing away at the peaks in this region is almost stunning.

A good description of this region was put together by Edward M. Taylor, a geologist at Oregon State University in Corvallis. In a guide to roadside geology, Taylor pointed out that this region of central Oregon "is chiefly a Pleistocene volcanic platform of overlapping basalt and basaltic andesite lava flows whose aggregate thickness is generally unknown, but probably exceeds 4,000 feet (1,200 meters) locally." He said this platform is elongated, perhaps 25 miles (40 kilometers) wide in some areas, and incredibly complex.

In short, he said, "the central High Cascade Range is not the simple . . . belt of andesite volcanoes commonly depicted in geology textbooks; instead it is a broad . . . platform of mafic composition in which open-textured lavas were at first predominant, then became subordinate to basaltic andesite."

Perhaps the most important idea proposed by Taylor is that the volcanoes situated between Mount Adams in the north and Mount Mazama to the south were created as a result of faulting action. He suggests that a huge graben some 20 miles (32 kilometers) wide may have dropped in that region, causing many fractures to open up and allow formation of volcanoes. As for the volcanoes that lie off the main axis of this fault system, it has been suggested that those like Mount St. Helens or the Newberry Crater in central Oregon may be situated on lateral faults associated with this down-thrust graben and fault system.

At first, back in about 1925, it was reported that the Three Sisters were probably once all part of one much larger single volcano. Later research, primarily by Howel Williams, indicated that each of the Three Sisters peaks is a separate volcano, with its own history and eruptive personality.

Oldest of the Three Sisters is the rugged, steep cone of North Sister, which stands some 10,000 feet (3,000 meters) tall and shows no evidence of a summit crater. Nonetheless, the mountain's base is 17 to 20 miles (22 to 31 kilometers) in diameter, and this suggests North Sister may once have stood as one of the tallest, most majestic mountains of the Cascade Range, at least 10,600 feet (3,200 meters) tall in its youth. It is thought that the cone may have been built in three distinct episodes, first as a wide basaltic shield formation, then as a taller cone constructed by relatively quiet lava flows, and finally as a tall fragmental cone created by a series of explosive eruptions. In the last stages, the summit cone was apparently filled by lava under pressure, which forced its way through fissures and cracks to build swarms of dikes. Since the cone has been so thoroughly eroded, these now stand out as stark lava walls radiating away from the summit area. Also at the summit is a huge brownish-green lava plug some 1,000 feet (300 meters) wide from which project two pinnacles, referred to as Middle and South Horns.

Top:
*Panoramic view, looking south,
shows the Three Sisters, in Oregon. (Oregon Army National
Guard photo)*

Bottom:
*The Three Sisters volcanic system,
as seen from the northeast.*

Smallest of the Three Sisters is Middle Sister, but it is only shorter than North Sister by about 40 feet (12 meters). It is a rather regular cone, except that one side, its east face, has been largely carried away, probably by glacial action.

South Sister, standing some 300 feet (90 meters) taller than North Sister, is the highest and the best preserved of the three, and it has retained its beautifully circular summit crater. Inside the crater a small lake forms in summer, creating the highest body of water in all of Oregon. This volcano is apparently built upon a basaltic shield volcano that produced pyroclastic eruptions. As a result, most of the cone is constructed of andesite and dacite. The geology of South Sister is marked by a series of massive obsidian domes that were extruded along the cone's southeastern base. The area is known for the sharp spires and large angular blocks that formed during eruptive phases.

There is something about 14,400-foot- (4,400-meter-) tall Mount Shasta that inspires thoughts of the supernatural. For some reason, Mount Shasta, more than any of the other Cascade volcanoes, has generated tales of strange peoples living inside a hollow, holy mountain. Mount St. Helens has always had Sasquach for its legend, but for some reason Shasta has drawn numerous religious and semireligious groups to its flanks, including the Rosicrucians, the Knights of the White Rose, the Radiant School of the Seekers and Servers, Understanding Inc., the I AM Foundation and others. Some of these groups believe that the mountain's supposedly hollow interior is home for the Lemurians, who are described as highly civilized refugees from something called the Kingdom of Mu, which is supposed to have submerged into the Pacific Ocean.

But even without the mythology, Mount Shasta is sufficiently fascinating in purely geological terms. It is, indeed, a beautifully formed stratovolcano by whose side is another large cone called Shastina. And, because it is so far south, just below the Oregon border in California, Mount Shasta has suffered very little from the erosional forces that have scraped and carved similarly massive peaks like Mount Rainier, Mount Hood, and Glacier Peak. Shasta, in fact, occupies a considerably drier environment than the other peaks, since the flow of moisture from the Pacific

The crater lake occupying the summit crater on South Sister.

Layers of colorful volcanic ash form the Painted Hills area of eastern Oregon.

Ocean is interrupted by the nearby Klamath Mountains. Mount Shasta does support a number of glaciers, but when compared to those dressing the more northern volcanic peaks, Shasta's glaciers are minuscule.

In terms of its eruptive history, Mount Shasta has produced considerably more material in the past few thousand years than have the volcanoes to the north. Since the last glaciation, Shasta has reclothed its flanks in fresh deposits of andesitic and dacitic lavas, along with pyroclastic flows. The mountain is believed to be made up of at least four cones that overlap. The oldest of the four—which originated more than 100,000 years ago—appears to be the structure now known as Sargeants Ridge on the south side of the cone. The next portion of the mountain to be built came from a new vent that broke out on the north flank of Sargeants Ridge. This eruption constructed a large cone of andesite lava, which is known as the Misery Hill volcano. This was then topped off with pumice flows near the summit vent.

Since then, in the past 12,000 years, the volcano has added both its present summit cone and the parasitic cone of Mount Shastina, which is located about half a mile to the west of the present Sisson Crater. After Shastina was built, activity apparently resumed on the larger mountain, near the main summit. There, the fourth major vent burst open north of the Misery Hill cone, producing some thick, blocky andesitic flows that built the Hotlum cone. At the summit crater, the rocky terrain is still stained a dirty yellow by a hot, sulphurous spring that flows from the base of a huge spire. It is thought that the eruptive activity that built the Hotlum cone occurred only a few thousand years ago and that the hot, acidic spring at the summit is good evidence that the dome is still cooling off. But there has been very little, if any, eruptive activity in historical times. Reports of steam eruptions being seen in the 1900s are difficult to document, and no traces of ash or other debris have been identified as having erupted recently. Temperature readings of the Mount Shasta summit area taken by the US Geological Survey, however, show anomalous hot spots. These, then, may represent areas where steam eruptions occurred more recently, as reported by early climbers who reached the summit.

Geologists believe that the eruptions that built Mount Shasta's large cone were probably very violent because deposits left by hot pyroclastic flows are still in evidence covering some 20 square miles (55 square kilometers) of land. This area includes the communities of Weed and Mount Shasta.

In addition to the Cascade volcanoes, Hawaii, the Aleutians, and Alaska, there are other areas in the United States where, over many thousands of years, the remnants of volcanism have been active in the form of steam vents, hot springs, and other phenomena. The most famous of these is Yellowstone National Park, where thousands of visitors stop to see the spectacular geysers, burping mud pots, hot springs, steam vents, and beautiful deposits of silica and carbonates that were put in place by hot water. These features, commonly considered the end stages of volcanic activity, mark zones where the heat from the earth's interior is causing changes on the surface.

Geologists who have worked the terrain in Yellowstone Park have noted that the youngest and most dominant volcanic eruptions produced rhyolite lavas, which are rich in silica, the volcanic equivalent of granite. In the distant past rhyolite eruptions were apparently quite common, and must have been among the most spectacular of natural phenomena. It is estimated that over 600 cubic miles (1,500 cubic kilometers) of rhyolite material erupted from the Yellowstone volcanoes alone in their last active periods. Two thirds of that amount erupted as ash flows similar to the River of Sand that produced the Valley of Ten Thousand Smokes in Alaska in 1912. In that ancient time, so great was the volume of such flows of pumice and ash that whole valleys were completely filled, with intervening ridges also being covered. As activity continued, these ash flows merged to form flat plateaus thousands of square kilometers in area.

Since these flows of ash were incredibly hot when deposited, their particles tended to fuse together to build a type of rock known as welded tuff. These rocks, according to fairly recent studies, are perhaps the most abundant rocks found in the western United States. In Nevada alone, for instance, there are tens of thousands of cubic miles of welded tuff. Similar huge deposits of welded tuff are found in the San Juan Mountains of Colorado, in New Mexico, in the Big Bend area of Texas, and in parts of Arizona.

This tells us, rather bluntly, that the West was really built by volcanoes. And, as Mount St. Helens now gives warning, construction is still in progress.

6 | *Ashfall*

Something did seem different when dark clouds gathered on the horizon that bright Sunday morning, but many farmers and stockmen thought it was just a bigger-than-usual thunderstorm moving in to drench fields and orchards with welcome moisture.

But then the dust came down, and Black Sunday was born.

The dust—fine, gritty ash from the massive eruption of Mount St. Helens—came billowing across the sky, spreading from the shattered volcano's cone toward the east and northeast, depositing a thickening blanket of talcum-fine particles onto everything. The thickest, most ash-rich part of Mount St. Helens's plume drifted with the wind across the beautiful, rich Yakima Valley, over Spokane, then across the eastern border of Washington into Idaho and Montana.

Hardest hit, apparently, were eight counties of eastern Washington, where annual agricultural production amounts to $1.4 billion in crops and some $270 million in livestock or the products from livestock. The most important crops there include fruit—especially the famous Washington delicious apples—hay, potatoes, cereal grains, and dry legumes (beans, peas, etc.). Other valuable but less important crops included hops for beer making, mint, and vegetable seeds.

In all, scientists estimated that from 1.7 to 2.4 billion cubic yards (1.5 to 2.0 cubic kilometers) of finely divided ash fell on farm, range, and forest land in a zone that included most of eastern Washington, much of Idaho, Montana, and even parts of the Dakotas and Canada. Later estimates indicated that almost 50 percent of the territory in Washington State received visible ashfall, and almost 30 percent of the state received ash deposits of more than 3 millimeters depth. The deepest deposits ranged from 50 to 80 millimeters (2 to 3 inches) deep. Eventually, however, this ash compacted, so that it occupied only about one-third of its original depth.

A report on how the ash spread was returned by Capt. Charles Rosenfeld, who was flying in an Oregon Army National Guard OV-1 Mohawk aircraft close to the huge volcanic plume just after the eruption began. He recalled,

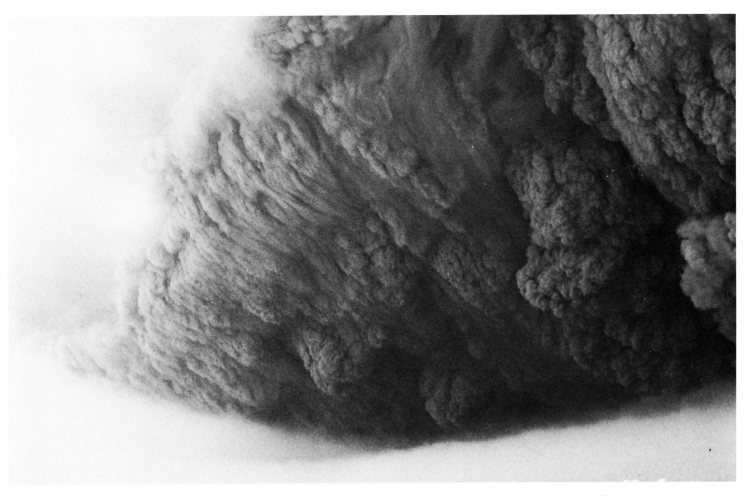

Dense Plinean ash plume can be seen moving from the right foreground toward the left background. Ash at lower levels obscures the view of the ground, while ash lifted into the stratosphere gives the sky a mottled appearance. The dense plume of ash appears to drip lobes of ash in places where cooler air has been entrained in the flow.

At 1 P.M. we climbed to 15,000 feet (4,700 meters) and skirted the eruption plume to the north of the mountain. The ground was still obscured by the rock chaff scattered by the initial lateral blast. The sun was hidden by the mottled stratosphere.

Between 25,000 and 40,000 feet (7,500 and 12,000 meters) we were facing a dense, ominously black cloud heavily laden with ash, pulsing its way to the east-northeast. It was a Plinean plume, acting as a gigantic conveyor belt. As it became cooler and denser with distance from the vent, the ash was gradually descending to the ground, beginning near Ritzville, Washington.

At the same time, too, some of the ash—that which had been blasted high into the stratosphere—began a journey that would carry it across the entire North American continent, across the east coast, the Atlantic Ocean, and eventually all the way around the world. According to Murray Mitchell, of the National Weather Service, the ash from Mount St. Helens that was injected into the statosphere completed its first trip around the globe in 17 days. In time, ash locked into the jet stream circulation patterns would thin and disappear, leaving scientists trying to calculate what, if any, the climatic effect had been.

Mitchell, speaking at a symposium seven months after the eruption, commented that "the consequences of the eruption (on the earth's climate) are so small that it will take a very sophisticated attempt to account for it."

On that first day, Black Sunday, however, in Yakima, Pullman and other communities—and even in Missoula, Montana—darkness came early, making everything, including agriculture, commerce, and road and air traffic, shut down. It was a terrifying time, a time of fear and prayers, of hope and despair, a time of too much to do and too little information.

Indeed, warnings of the coming ash cloud were largely ineffective. Studies done in the wake of the eruption and ashfall by Thomas Downing and James Lyons, of Clark University in Massachusetts, indicated the ashfall was first mistaken for a thunderstorm, "and few people were really aware of the ashfall hazards. It wasn't at first perceived as a hazard, and effective warnings were not forthcoming," Downing said.

In the town of Cheney, for example, he added, the police dispatcher posted the ashfall warning on a bulletin board, but did not spread the word farther, thinking the ashfall would not be serious.

In Missoula, Montana, information was scarce, and people who wanted to know what was going on and what to do got their best advice by telephoning the sheriff's office. Most other information sources were either uninformed, tardy with the information, or misleading.

As ash began accumulating like unmeltable snow, travelers in eastern Washington became stranded and were soon herded off the hazardous roads by police and highway emergency crews. Then, as the ash blanket deepened, homeowners, shopkeepers, and public employees began shoveling it off the roofs, afraid that rain, if it came, would mix with ash to form a heavy, roof-cracking slurry that might quickly harden into concrete.

Technical Vignette: Mount St. Helens tephra and its composition
Alan N. Federman

Explosive eruptions of volcanoes produce pyroclastic materials. The word pyroclastic comes from the Greek, for "fire-broken." Any such material moved through the air, regardless of size or composition, is called tephra. And tephra can further be classified according to size and composition.

Microscopic examination of Mount St. Helens tephra, using sand-size particles or smaller, reveals three basic compositional groups: glasses, crystals, and lithic fragments.

The lithics are rock fragments that were broken up by the force of the eruption. Most of these fragments are volcanic in nature and represent previous lava flows, dikes and domes that solidified in the volcano's past history. And, as might be expected from the extremely explosive nature of Mount St. Helens's May 18, 1980, eruption, a great deal of this material is present in the ash. Also, because its composition is so similar to the molten magma responsible for the eruption, distinguishing between the two is not a trivial task.

Molten magma is typically a mixture of liquids, crystals, and sometimes gases that exists within the earth. The special case that interests us here involves a mass of magma that has accumulated somewhere near the earth's surface, such as under the volcano. Although the magma is a complex mixture, the bulk of its composition can be explained in about a dozen rather common chemical elements. And since oxygen is the most common of these elements, most geologists list the composition of the rock, mineral, or magma according to the oxides of the most common elements.

In approximate order of abundance of oxides by percentage of weight, as determined by an instrument called a microprobe analyzer, were the oxides of silicon (71.5 percent), aluminum (14.7 percent), sodium (5.10 percent), calcium (2.2 percent), iron (2 percent), potassium (1.9 percent), magnesium (0.5 percent), and titanium (0.3 percent). And in explosive episodes of volcanism, the gas phase—usually water in the form of superheated steam—is also very important. Indeed, its rapid expansion is usually the main reason for the violence of the eruptions.

The study of crystals can give clues to the temperature and other conditions present in the body of magma. When ice crystals are found growing on the surface of a pond, for example, the temperature of the water must be 0°C. Similarly, studying the kinds and chemical compositions of the glass and crystals present in the ashfall offers clues about the original magma.

As it turns out, glass was the major liquid portion of the Mount St. Helens magma just prior to the eruption. Quick chilling in the atmosphere has frozen this material with gas bubbles still intact. The chemical composition of the glass and the temperature just prior to eruption determine, to a certain degree, the shape and form of the small glass fragments. The fragments are usually referred to as glass or pumice shards.

Crystals, of course, are present in all rocks, and may actually be lithics. To determine unambiguously whether a crystal coexisted with the liquid, only those with rims of glass should be studied.

Face masks, some just makeshift pieces of cloth, were *de rigeur* for anyone going outdoors who hoped to avoid breathing the tiny, irritating dust particles. Real concern arose for the health of people living in an atmosphere thick with fine gray ash, and hospitals braced for an onslaught of respiratory emergencies. It was not known how dangerous the particles might be for those who breathed them. According to tests run by the US Center for Disease Control, however, the ash was not especially dangerous in terms of its chemistry, being almost neutral, and it did not appear to be a cause of the chronic lung disease known as silicosis. Free silica may cause silicosis in humans, but even if there is as much as 10 percent free silica, the danger to humans and animals is still quite low. It was noted that years of exposure to high concentrations of the dust would be required before serious health effects were seen.

As it turned out, the earliest, most obvious victims of the widespread ashfall were motor vehicles, many of which soon ground to a halt, immobilized by air filters clogged with dust. Governor Dixy Lee Ray observed that within one or two days of the ashfall more than half the cars operated by state police, local police, and emergency agencies were out of service. Some of the mechanical failures also included automatic transmissions that were damaged by the abrasive ash particles. Efforts to cope with such problems included building makeshift ducting systems to draw less dusty air from auto passenger compartments, snorkellike intake pipes on auto engines to draw air from above the highway dust cloud, and simply cleaning out auto engine air filters every few miles. None of these schemes worked too well, since the dust was so ubiquitous, but they may have extended the range and lifetime of some vehicles.

In addition, airplanes were grounded, trains halted, and truck traffic stopped in much of western Washington. For awhile it seemed that food distribution systems and other basic services would break down completely.

Yet the greatest concern—other than for the health of people—was what the ashfall might do to agriculture. Almost everyone in eastern Washington, either directly or indirectly, makes a living off the crops that thrive in the region's rich volcanic soils, and the crops were being buried in ash. The depth of the ash blanket varied considerably in agricultural areas to the east of Mount St.

Helens, ranging from some 50 millimeters (2 inches) deep within 30 miles (50 kilometers) of the mountain to about 20 millimeters (1 inch) deep in Yakima and the neighboring communities of Selah, Union Gap, and Moxee City.

Some optimists, of course, suggested hopefully that the addition of fine ash to the soils might actually be beneficial, putting in a few chemicals that would be good for plant growth. Chemical analysis of the ash discounted that idea, however, since the ash's agriculturally useful chemicals are not readily liberated by any known soil activity. In addition, the ash contains no organic matter—of such great importance to soil fertility. Indeed, the addition of large amounts of sterile ash to the soil actually decreases the percentage of organic matter present, creating problems rather than solving them.

Another research team looking at the impact of the ashfall on agriculture—a team made up of experts from the US Department of Agriculture and from Washington State—reported their findings in the January 2, 1981, issue of *Science*, the journal published by the American Association for the Advancement of Science (AAAS). They summarized their findings in these words:

Ash from Mt. St. Helens has fallen over a diverse agricultural area, with deposits up to 30 kilograms per square meter. Crop losses in eastern Washington are estimated at about $100 million in 1980—about 7 percent of the normal crop value in the affected area and less than was expected initially.

Production of wheat, potatoes and apples will be normal or above normal because the favorable conditions for growth of these crops since the ashfall helped offset the losses. Alfalfa hay was severely lodged under the weight of the ash, but ash-contaminated hay is apparently non-toxic when eaten by livestock.

The ash, as an abrasive, is apparently lethal to certain insects such as bees and grasshoppers, but populations are recovering. The ash has increased crop production costs by necessitating machinery repairs and increased tillage.

On soil, the ash reduces water infiltration, increases surface albedo, and may continue to affect water runoff, erosion, evaporation and soil temperature when tilled into the soil.

Ash on plant leaves reduced photosynthesis by up to 90 percent. Most plants have tended to shed the ash. With the possible exception of sulfur, the elements in the ash are either unavailable or present in very low concentrations; and no significant contribution to the nutrient status of soils is expected.

Lyons, from Clark University, added that for farmers, "as the ash began to fall, it became evident that this was abnormal, and they began taking steps to protect their livestock and their equipment."

Early advice from agricultural experts, unfortunately, tended to be conflicting, so that the farmers found themselves essentially on their own. Within a short time, however, "the farmers became the experts on coping. They had to to it on a day-to-day basis," but they learned fast and did manage to minimize the damage in most instances, Lyons said.

Lyons and Downing discussed their findings during a symposium on Mount St. Helens at the annual meeting of the AAAS held in January, 1981, in Toronto, Canada. They noted, for instance, that the timing of the eruption and ashfall was crucial. For instance, because pollination of the area's crop of red delicious apples had already been completed by the time of the eruption, the only thing that the apple growers had to do was somehow dust the ash off the trees' leaves so that photosynthesis wouldn't be hampered and the leaves wouldn't get sunburned. Some growers tried blowing the dust off by flying helicopters over their orchards. Later they used groundbased blowing machines. Then they turned on wind machines that are normally used for frost protection. In the end, many growers turned to tall sprinklers to wash the last of the ash from their trees' leaves. As it turned out, rainfall in the region was 20 to 25 percent above normal, which helped wash plants free of the dust and helped alleviate the dust problem in general.

It was reported, however, that some apple orchards in the Yakima Valley, where some of the earliest harvesting occurs, experienced some abnormal fruit drop after the ashfall. This was thought to be attributable in part to reduction of the rate of photosynthesis while the leaves were ash covered.

Even worse, a large apple orchard near Royal Slope, in Grant County, suffered 75-percent fruit drop from red delicious trees and a 5- to 10-percent drop from golden delicious trees. Tree leaves in this orchard, however, had been covered with ash to depths of up to 30 millimeters (1 inch) right after the eruption on May 18.

Alfalfa farmers—as mentioned by the other research team—were not as fortunate as most of the apple growers. Their crops, which had already become lush and green, almost ready for the first cutting of the spring, were laid low—lodged—by the weight of the ash. The impact on this crop was severe, probably amounting to losses as high as $35 million. In fact, most of the alfalfa crop was lost, and growers who tried to harvest it anyway found their hay laden with dust. Even though it was still edible by livestock, the loses were substantial.

For alfalfa farmers it became a question of starting over—either plowing the alfalfa under and then reseeding or simply cutting the existing crop and waiting for the next. Those whose alfalfa—a perennial crop—had already been in the ground a few years generally chose to plow it under and reseed. Farmers who had recently reseeded, however, usually chose to keep the plants and wait for the next cutting. By July 1, some 12,000 acres (5,000 hectares) of alfalfa in Grant County alone had been plowed under.

Wheat farmers, in contrast, did well. Their plants had not yet "headed out," and the ash on the ground apparently acted as a mulch, conserving moisture in the soil. Since the wheat plants were still relatively short and stiff, they resisted lodging and the ash that accumulated on the leaves apparently fell off easily and coated the ground, providing the new mulch. In a few areas, however, the ash apparently also increased the rate of water runoff, causing minor problems. Still, in the end, the wheat harvest turned out to be a bumper crop, perhaps even a record.

Some favorite fruits for canning and the table—such as peaches and apricots—also suffered significant losses. Since these fruits have skins that are covered with very find hairs, or fuzz, they are difficult to clean of ash, and a high percentage of crop dusted by the May 18 eruption could not be sold.

Raspberries in northern Oregon—which were hit by ash after the June 12 ashfall—were also unacceptable for processing, so about 75 percent of this crop was lost. Also, about 40 percent of the strawberry crop in southwestern Washington and Oregon was lost because of ash dusting from the June 12 event. The ash apparently forced the strawberry plants' leaves down, pressing the fruit onto the soil, where the strawberries rotted. Blueberries

Homestead near Moses Lake, Washington, smothered by heavy ashfall. Cattle ranchers hastily improvised temporary feedlots to keep the herds from swallowing large amounts of silica that covered the plants on their normal rangeland.

in western Washington were nearing maturity when the wet ash-fall of May 25 hit. The fruit was damaged and became unmarketable.

The team made up of representatives of the USDA—R. J. Cook and J. C. Barron—and Washington State—R. I. Papendick and G. J. Williams III—commented in their *Science* article that "the full impact of the eruptions on the soils and on the plant and animal life where ash fell will never be known and even now is mostly speculation. [But] initial estimates that losses to crops and livestock would be large have been revised downward." They added, however, that the ash must now be considered a permanent addition to the land.

This addition to the soil, they noted, is made up mostly of pulverized dacitic and andesitic rock fragments and volcanic glass, which has a consistency similar to dry portland cement, and appeared to accumulate in two distinct layers. The first layer was a medium-gray color, while the following deposit was a paler gray, almost white. It was suggested that the lower layer may contain volcanic rock from Mount St. Helens's older structures, such as the crater wall, the dome or the vents. The lighter-colored ash is thought to have come from new magma that welled up from deep within the earth. The particles themselves tend to be jagged crystals ranging in diameter between one tenth of a micron (one millionth of a meter) to 500 microns.

Among the most seriously affected victims of the eruption were the area's insects. Most of the damage to the insect population was attributed to ash particles' tendency to abrade the waxy protective layer on the outside of insects' stiff hides, their cuticles. Once this barrier is breached, too much moisture escapes from insects' bodies and they die. Also, the insects' ability to fly was impaired by the ash that collected on their bodies, further endangering the numerous species in the area of ashfall.

Some of the insects killed by the ashfall were pests—including grasshoppers and the Colorado potato beetle. The ash-kill of grasshoppers was so effective, when combined with cool, wet climatic conditions, that normal spraying for grasshopper control was canceled. A year earlier, 32,000 acres (130,000 hectares) of crop and grasslands had been sprayed for grasshopper control.

On the other hand, unfortunately, the beneficial species of insects—including honey and pollinating bees, several types of wasps, and yellowjackets—were the hardest hit by the ashfall. It was estimated, in fact, that out of 15,000 bee colonies in the irrigated Columbia Basin, 12,000 were either destroyed or severely damaged. Losses to honey bees and pollinating bees were later estimated at $1 million, but it was soon noted that the populations of bees in the stricken area were beginning to rebound.

Since the ashfall, concern has also arisen about the increased reflectivity of the soil. It was noted by Lyons and Downing at the Toronto meeting of the AAAS, for example, that increased brightness of the soil, with light-colored ash on the surface, had reduced peak soil temperatures in some areas by as much as 18°F (10°C), causing some just emerging crops to go dormant. In response, some farmers quickly tilled the soil, turning the ash under, thereby darkening the soil so that it absorbed more heat from the sun.

The ash is also thought to decrease the permeability of the soil to both air and water. Since the ash particles are so fine—about 2 microns in diameter—they tend to plug the larger pores in the soil, forming blockades where water was earlier able to flow. Because of this effect, the surface layer of ash is expected to slow evaporation of water from the soil, keeping the subsurface moisture content higher for longer periods. At the same time, however, this blockage will tend to increase runoff and keep some water from percolating into the soil.

This runoff problem may become severe. There is real concern that increased resistance to the flow of water into the ground may greatly increase the amount of surface runoff in wet periods. The result, of course, would be increased danger from floods and mudflows, plus a large increase in the rate of soil erosion. And since the ash is so loose, so transportable either by wind or water, the problem of rapid sedimentation of reservoirs and other standing bodies of water may become severe.

What all this means is that the Pacific Northwest's rich agricultural lands have been changed—but not disastrously so. The soils will remain rich and productive, and agriculture will continue as the dominant source of income. But there may well be some problems.

7 | *Life around the Volcano*

"One thing you don't want to do," James Sedell said, "is try walking upstream at night." Pushed-over trees poking up through the mud "are like bayonets, sandblasted and honed needle-sharp. It's really treacherous."

In some places these sharpened treetops represent all that is left of the once lush forests that stood tall and majestic along canyon walls and adjacent to streambeds draining water off beautiful Mount St. Helens. But all that changed drastically, quickly. The mountain and its neighborhood were cataclysmically transformed into a stark gray desert where, months later, a few tufts of green were slowly emerging from the thick cover of ash, rock, and mud.

Sedell, a specialist in aquatic ecology at the US Forest Service's Pacific Northwest Forest and Range Experiment Station, had been out on the mountain and around its flanks in the weeks and months following the massive eruption of the volcano, studying the ecological damage and the reemergence of life in the devastated debris flows and ash deposits.

In addition to wildlife, of course, there were people out there on the mountain, and none of them could have been ready for the hot blast of steam, ash, and dust that came storming down the mountain's sides on the morning of May 18, 1980.

Of the people who were trapped too close to the volcano, at least a few must have thought they might outrace the broiling-hot cascade of ash, gas, and rock debris by speeding away in cars or trucks. Most perished in a matter of minutes, quickly overtaken by the dark gray cloud that some scientists estimate carried temperatures above 600°F (300°C) and moved well in excess of 100 miles (160 kilometers) per hour.

Some victims were found dead in or near their vehicles; others were never seen again, having probably been buried in the deep, hot blanket of light-gray, powdery ash that quickly covered everything. Buried along with these human victims, of course, were uncountable numbers of wild animals, birds, and other creatures that had lived as part of a complex forest community on the flanks of the big volcano. In many areas the forest itself was gone, the ground stripped completely bare. Many of the trees that remained had been stripped naked of branches, bark, and leaves, laid flat, then buried yards deep in a pressure cooker of hot ash.

This, then, is what the first observers saw when they ventured into the danger zone in a frantic search for survivors. Rivers and streams, choked and overflowing with mud and ash, continued belching clouds of steam and dust as trickles of water contacted hot ash, creating superheated steam that quickly exploded, flashing up through the gray surface shroud of ash.

Since then, researchers have calculated that surface temperatures in the danger zone, in the 200-square-mile (550-square-kilometer) area demolished by the eruption of Mount St. Helens, must have reached more than 600°F (320°C) within the first few minutes of the ash cloud's arrival. Temperatures subsided to about 350°F (180°C) for the next few hours before finally cooling to more normal levels.

Below the surface, however, it was a different story. The ash deposited by the eruption acted as a very good insulating material, so that only tens of centimeters beneath the surface the material remained hot—very hot—for months after the eruption.

Dr. Stanley H. Zisk, a planetary scientist at the Haystack Radio Astronomy Observatory in Massachusetts, and other researchers flew in by helicopter to examine an ash flow several months after the eruption. Dr. Zisk noted that they found the ash still incredibly hot just a small distance beneath the surface.

"We found the strangest phenomenon, too," he recalled in an interview. "If you stepped on the ash, you immediately sank in quite deeply, and you could get a pretty bad burn. But if you put your foot lightly onto the surface, then shook it, the ash seemed to solidify—enough so it would support your weight and you could walk on it. But when you came back across the ash field, you had to walk in your previous footprints. Then it was safe."

In our own experience on those ash fields, we walked around rather blithely, unaware at first how hot it was beneath the surface. But when we shoved a temperature probe down to a depth of about 1 meter, and hooked up the wires, the temperature reading jumped immediately to 600°F (300°C). We jumped back into the helicopter quickly.

Pointy-stick zone where trees, pushed over by the huge mudflows, were worn needle sharp by abrasion (US Forest Service photo by Fred Swanson)

Another researcher, Dr. Richard J. Janda, pointed out that beneath these incredibly hot beds of ash there is a great amount of buried wood and other organic debris that has been thoroughly cooked—pyrolized. Janda, a US Geological Survey employee who took up a new station in Vancouver, Washington, after the Mount St. Helens eruption, said this cooking action apparently created many exotic chemicals that were later found to be draining out of the ash, contaminating water in the lakes and ponds that were accumulating in the danger zone. Speaking at the annual meeting of the AAAS held in Toronto, Canada, Janda said the chemicals that are finding their way out from under the ash include a large amount of compounds called phenols, which are made from "steam-blasted wood."

Sedell, with the US Forest Service, in addition emphasized that a tremendous amount of organic material was buried beneath the ash. He noted that most of the conifers in the blast and debris zone had been just on the verge of bursting forth with their spring foliage, meaning that each tree was lush with the resins and juices of spring, ready for a new burst of growth. As these materials were baked out of the tree trunks, branches, leaves, and other materials that were locked in the ash, they began seeping into the lakes, ponds, and streams that formed in the debris flows. The result was an unusually rich stew of organic chemicals showing up in the surface waters.

Before the eruption, of course, these streams and rivers had been cold, clear, and turbulent, cascading down over mossy boulders and old tree trunks, providing a richly diversified habitat for organisms—and a wonderland for fishermen. After the eruption, however, such waterways were buried and/or cooked in the pyroclastic flows that came roaring down the mountain. The streams remaining were choked with floating chunks of pumice and laden with thick deposits of ash and woody organic debris. The water became a thick brown-gray soup, and no signs of life remained.

Soon, however, even within two weeks of the massive eruption, communities of filamentous bacteria and even blue-green algae were discovered growing abundantly at the edges of waterways and in backwater areas of what had once been the beautiful North Toutle River. These organisms apparently were taking advantage of this rich abundance of chemicals—these complex

organic chemicals—being leached into the streams from the shattered rocks and trees buried in the thick ashflows.

Farther downstream on the western side of the mountain, however, where massive mudflows had completely obliterated the normal channels of the North Toutle River and the Cowlitz River, the waters remained so thick with gritty ash that adult salmon could only survive a few hours before the sharp sedimentary particles sliced up their fragile gills. It was through these channels on the western side of the mountain where, after the big blast, a 45-mile- (70-kilometer)-long mudflow came rushing down to pour water and mud, at temperatures up to 85°F (32°C), into the Columbia River. This hot flow eliminated almost all forms of life from the smaller rivers.

Sedell noted that in the streams and rivers suffocated by ash, the abundance and diversity of living organisms will probably continue to be sparse until after the ash has been transported downstream to the sea. The valuable spawning grounds and rearing pools once used by the salmon fishery were totally destroyed, buried in ash. But, Sedell said, in time—perhaps even within one decade—the waters of the Toutle River should recover sufficiently to maintain healthy runs of salmon and steelhead trout. How soon this may happen will depend, of course, on the mountain's eruptive activity settling down.

It was noted, too, that some of the tributary streams that flow into the ash-clogged rivers served as major refuges for fish outside the blast zone. Other fish found refuge in some of the smaller new ponds and lakes formed when the massive mudflows dammed the smaller streams. These new lakes, in turn, then acted as settling basins for the ash, allowing it to be deposited as sediment before the water moved on downstream.

On the eastern side of the mountain, in contrast, the streams were affected rather differently. These tributaries, even though hit by heavy ashfalls, apparently were able to maintain relatively intact communities of insects and fish, including members of the salmon family. These fish did show signs of their gills being abraded, but they seemed to be surviving. In addition, their habitat—including rearing ponds—still existed, so that recovery of the fish population was expected to be relatively rapid in such areas.

Sedell also reported that the impact of the eruption of Mount St. Helens on lakes and streams differed from that of well-studied volcanic eruptions in Russia, Alaska, and Japan. The difference, he said, was probably because a rich forest surrounded Mount St. Helens, allowing the blast to deposit tremendous quantities of organic matter into the different bodies of water. Indeed, Sedell said researchers have found that the organic matter in the lakes increased 20- to 200-fold following the eruption and that the woody debris along all shorelines was up to 100 times greater. Streams and rivers, in fact, were transporting hundreds upon hundreds of tons of broken wood, branches, bark, and burnt foliage downstream toward the Columbia River and the sea.

In the blast area, Sedell said, more than 30 lakes were directly affected by the big explosion of May 18. Where these lake waters had once been quite low in nutrients, and renowned for their sparkling, crystal-clear waters, they quickly turned black, or cloudy green and brown. The coloring seemed to depend both on the size of the lakes and on how far they were from the erupting mountain. Spirit Lake, for example, was formerly a beautifully picturesque lake situated very close to Mount St. Helens. But it very quickly turned deep black, stained by the leaching chemicals from cooking trees and foliage.

Sedell and his coworkers in Oregon, Jerry Franklin and Frederick Swanson, writing in *American Forests*, the magazine of the American Forestry Association, put it this way:

Biological recovery of Spirit Lake and the newly-formed lakes has begun from scratch. These lakes, filled with debris, could be described as "primordial soup." A foul odor from burning wood, turpentine and sulfur rises from Spirit Lake. Micro-organisms flourish as large populations of bacteria, algae and protozoans feed upon each other and upon the rich reservior of dissolved nutrients.

Mosquitos are rapidly colonizing the lakes. The biological production of Spirit Lake has never been higher—although it has thus far been limited to single-cell organisms.

The small ponds in the debris flow of the North Toutle River changed color in a few days from murky green to red-brown as different algal and bacterial flora took over.

In addition, they wrote, the lakes within the area where whole forests of timber were blown down soon became dominated by

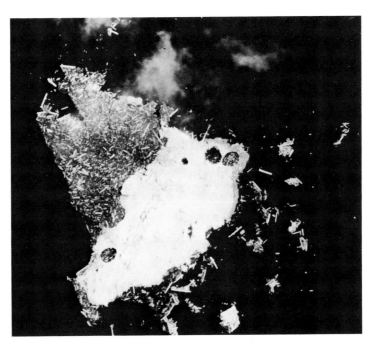

A new island in Spirit Lake, consisting of debris from the May 18 eruption, is pockmarked as a result of explosions forming craters. The lake's waters, once blue and clear, have been turned black by the growth of algae.

filamentous and spiral bacteria. But they also sustained diverse communities of plants and animals, including other bacteria, zooplankton, and bottom-dwelling animals, along with salamanders and crayfish. Indeed, they said, "considering the physical damage to surrounding forests, the aquatic communities are surprisingly intact. Hellgammites and stoneflies emerged within weeks of the eruption, and are now numerous."

Given time, too, they said, the bottoms of the lakes—which were completely depleted of dissolved oxygen—should recover sufficiently to support fish populations, perhaps even within a few years.

As for the vegetation, Sedell and others reported that even before the ash stopped falling, the green tint of surviving plants was becoming visible in the gray blanket. But the blast from the volcano had, almost instantly, killed all plant growth above ground. Nonetheless, in most areas the blast, heat, and ash did not sterilize the soil, so that plants began sprouting from the roots or rhizomes within just a matter of weeks, while fireweed—which seems well adapted to such conditions—pushed through the crust of ash. And where erosion was removing all or part of the ash and pumice, regrowth became particularly vigorous.

Indeed, as the weeks passed the community of plants that began revegetating the denuded slopes became more diverse, and wetlands such as marshes began standing out as bright green patches in an ocean of gray. It was reported that areas near the mountain that had previously been "clear cut" in timbering operations seemed to rebound fastest, with fireweed, blackberries, and other herbaceous plants coming back strongly.

In some areas where snow cover had existed at the time of the blast, tree trunks had been scorched down to the level at which the snow had melted, but below that the stumps were intact, and the roots of some plants were still alive and had begun throwing up vigorous new shoots, starting life over again. The snowpack had also protected some shrubs and small trees from the hot flow of gas and debris and, as it melted and slumped, it tended to break up the crust of ash to provide routes for regrowth of plants. And so, in some protected areas a kind of instant forest began emerging.

By late summer, foresters report, natural reseeding of the blast zone began in earnest with the arrival of fireweed, pearly everlasting, and other light and far-traveling seeds. Many plants were sprouting in rills by summer's end, including the ferns, huckleberry, and trillium, and even on the mudflows of the Toutle and Muddy rivers seedlings of black cottonwood were growing vigorously.

Wildlife had also been decimated by the eruption. Nonetheless, soon after the eruption observers encountered the tracks of deer, elk, coyotes, and other larger creatures that somehow had survived the blast. Most conspicuous, however, were the insects and other small creatures, including large numbers of foraging ants, flies, hornets, and hosts of mosquitoes. It is thought that burrowing animals such as pocket gophers and moles also survived in large numbers.

One of the most vexing questions remaining was what to do with all the very large, very valuable trees that had been blown down. Foresters concluded that a large amount of the lumber could be saved if it was hauled out and sliced up within two, or even four, years. There was some debate, however, over how much of the wood should be removed. Sedell, giving a seminar at the Woods Hole Oceanographic Institution in Massachusetts, remarked that "the question involves that big wood. It's good, and it can be salvaged. But as a biologist I'd like to leave it there because it's providing really diverse habitat and deflecting stream flow. I think they can probably take some of it, but we've been putting a lot of effort" into leaving some of the timber on the ground.

Sedell, noting that the foresters "figure they've got about four years to get it out" before it deteriorates too far, "before it starts getting worked over by beetles," reported that the private timber harvesters were already moving fast, and that "on the Green River, and on the North Fork of the Toutle, about 300 logging trucks per day were moving out of there. There are about 80 tons of trees on each load, and it's expected there will be 600 trucks per day by the end of the year. So there's a tremendous flow of wood" coming from the blown-down forest.

This was possible, he added, because the Weyerhauser Company's timber roads "were basically left intact," and the roads into the timberlands on other private land also made the blown-

The initial explosion left this crater gaping in the peak of Mount St. Helens. It is clearly flanked by fracture zones crossing the peak.

Below:
Photograph taken on April 10 illustrates the dramatic inflation of the bulge area.

Above right:
Looking down from the northeast, at 8:32 A.M. on May 18, Keith and Dorothy Stoffel shot this picture of rock and ice avalanching down into the Mount St. Helens crater. At the lower right, a burst of steam escapes from a fissure that is opening up just below the false summit. This is the beginning of the earthquake-triggered slide. (Photo: Keith and Dorothy Stoffel)

Bottom right:
The landslide begins its massive flow down the mountain's north flank, while the first projectiles from the huge lateral blast erupt out of the exposed side plane near the center of The Bulge. The base of the slide can be seen cascading down toward the Toutle Valley on the right. (Photo: Keith and Dorothy Stoffel)

Below:
The furious eruption bursts through the summit as the landslide, lower right, uncovers the zone of superheated groundwater in the mountain. Visible here are three components of the initial blast: the lateral blast from the slide plane, a large eruption throwing huge projectiles northward, and the near-vertical explosion from the summit crater. (Photo: Keith and Dorothy Stoffel)

Right:
Mount St. Helens's massive eruption plume, as seen from 6 miles (10 kilometers) south of the shattered mountain just after the beginning of the May 18, 1980, eruption. A ring of condensation clouds shrouds the crater rim, probably a result of the initial explosion.

Left:
The breached, wide-open crater created by the landslide and explosion of May 18.

Below left:
View of the breached north side of Mount St. Helens, taken from the northwest shore of Spirit Lake. The large blocks of rock seen in the foreground were thrown to their present locations by the large explosive eruption, a lateral blast, that occurred on May 18, 1980.

Below right:
Chaotically strewn remnants of a shattered forest, covered with blast deposits and ash, can be seen to the northeast of Mount St. Helens.

Right:
Dr. Robert Ballard, from the Woods Hole Oceanographic Institution in Massachusetts, inspects one of the first specimens of giant tube worms found living around hydrothermal vents on the seafloor, near the Galapagos Islands. (Photo by Jack Donnelly, WHOI)

Far right:
Using the submarine Alvin, scientists dove down to the seafloor off the west coast of Mexico, where they found chimneys emitting extremely hot, metal-rich plumes of water. This black smoker was among the hottest, and its chimney was apparently built up by deposition of sulfide minerals leached from seafloor rocks.

Mount Hood, Oregon, as seen from the south.

Below:
Successive layers of thin flood basalts are clearly exposed in the walls of the Columbia River Gorge at Rowena, Oregon.

Right:
Charles Rosenfeld examines the surface of a fresh pahoehoe lava flow on the flanks of the Kilauea volcano on the island of Hawaii.

down wood accessible. On US Forest Service lands, however, access to the downed timber was more difficult, making harvest of the wood slower.

Throughout this period—as the trees were being trucked away, as the forest clean-up efforts began, as the bridges and roads were being reopened—there was the problem of massive erosion. There was also the danger of large, devastating mudflows pouring down the Toutle River, into the Cowlitz River, and again into the Columbia River, inundating the towns of Kelso and Longview with mud.

Dick Janda, of the Geological Survey, warned bluntly eight months after the major eruption that a vast, dangerous flood of muddy water could come down toward these two towns at any time. In fact, Janda warned that "if I lived in Kelso or Longview, I'd keep my ear on the radio all the time." He noted that the US Army Corps of Engineers may have underestimated the amount of mud, water, and debris that could break loose at higher elevations, and he pointed out that two small dams that the corps had built to contain the flow of muddy water had already failed. As it turned out, the Geological Survey and the Corps of Engineers had released two very different estimates of the flood hazard. According to the Geological Survey, 500 million cubic yards (400 million cubic meters) of muddy water could flow; the Corps of Engineers estimated that between 15 and 30 million cubic yards (12 and 25 million cubic meters) of mud-rich water might move down the channels.

Two of the corps's dams—one on the North Toutle River, and a smaller one on the South Toutle River—had already been damaged by early winter rains, with the promise of more damage to come. These dams were built on each fork of the Toutle River in an attempt to relieve the flowing water of its load of debris and mud. The rockfill and gravel structures were designed to let the water filter through while slowing the flow to allow suspended sediments to settle out. In addition, nine sediment basins were built along the river—downstream from the catch dams—to capture any sediment that filtered through the dams.

Captain Michael Adams, with the Corps of Engineers' Portland, Oregon, office, explained that "every pound of mud we can wring from the stream will reduce the danger of flooding downstream.

We know there's lots more mud up there. The May 18 eruption flattened 150 square miles of timber and left the area susceptible to erosion."

In anticipation of worse weather and a growing hazard from flooding, the Corps of Engineers hired 28 contractors to work two 10-hour shifts per day, 6 days a week, on 22 pipeline dredges and 49 draglines to try to clear channels for the water, mud, and debris yet to come. By early November they were removing close to half a million cubic yards (350,000 cubic meters) of sediment and debris daily along the Toutle, Cowlitz, and Columbia rivers. The goal set by the Corps of Engineers was to clear the mighty Columbia River of about 20 million cubic yards (15 million cubic meters) of debris-laden sediments by the end of November and finish dredging about 40 million cubic yards (35 million cubic meters) from the Cowlitz River by sometime in December.

In addition to the dredging and channel-clearing work, the corps had contracted for increasing the height of almost 6 miles (10 kilometers) of levees and construction of close to 6,500 feet (2,000 meters) of new levees along the Cowlitz River. The Toutle River was being sealed close to its confluence with the Cowlitz. Engineers were using a series of debris barriers and basins in an effort to block the flow of sediments into the larger downstream rivers.

Such major work was necessary because after Mount St. Helens erupted, some 30 million cubic meters of mud and woody debris had been deposited in the Cowlitz River, reducing its flow capacity by about 85 percent. This, in the event of even a moderate rainstorm, would threaten serious flooding for the 45,000 people who lived in three downstream communities.

The Corps of Engineers said it planned additionally to award 15 new dredging contracts over the winter and expected to spend $80 million through 1981 in maintaining the channels and levees built in the first phase of construction. "Historically," Janda explained, "the largest-magnitude floods are those generated by warm tropical storms" that drop rain on beds of snow. This most often occurs in December and January. Fortunately, however, snowpack on the mountainside was relatively light during that first winter after the blast.

Right:
As a result of the blast from Mount St. Helens, millions of tons of easily moved sediment have been stored in the huge debris avalanche that swept down to clog the North Toutle River valley.

Below:
Coldwater Lake, formed as the creek was dammed by the debris flow that clogged the North Toutle River valley.

On Christmas Day the area got a taste of what might come later. With snowpack averaging 8 inches (20 centimeters) of water equivalent, the warm rains came. The runoff quickly peaked by the morning of December 26, and the large retention dam on the North Fork of the Toutle River became heavily packed with a dense, turbid mixture of mud, water, and shattered timber. The spillway, which had been lined with rock-filled gabions, was unable to withstand the erosive nature of the viscous flood and soon failed. This allowed the muddy water to race downstream unchecked, where the abrasive flow further eroded the damaged streambanks, even endangering the large bridge carrying US Interstate Highway 5.

Thus the North Toutle Dam lay in ruins, the flood having carved a large gash through its center span, washing away much of the 9.5 million cubic yards (7.5 million cubic meters) of sediment that had earlier been trapped behind it. It was fortunate that this flood was relatively small. If it had come during a winter of normal precipitation, when snowpack would be considerably deeper, the North Fork dam might have ruptured suddenly, releasing a tremendous amount of water to go cascading down the canyons into the valley below.

Much concern was also focused on a huge pile of ash, mud, and other debris that had formed a large new dam blocking Coldwater Creek. A lake containing as much as 100,000 acre-feet of water had built up behind the dam, and it was not known whether the barrier was sufficiently strong to hold very long. Janda shared this concern. He noted that since so much loose material was distributed by the massive eruption of Mount St. Helens, the whole area was very, very erodable and unstable. And Sedell remarked in his talk at Woods Hole that the water running off the mountain was so loaded with ash and mud that "it's just like liquid stone flowing down the valley." Some streams, he remarked, had very quickly cut deep ravines into the soft ash and mud, and some had cut all the way down below their preblast streambeds in less than eight months' time.

Technical Vignette: Erosion
Charles Rosenfeld

During the first hours and days following the massive May 18 eruption of Mount St. Helens, the flow of ash from the volcano that settled over much of the Pacific Northwest began to pose a serious erosion problem. The problem became most noticeable, first, in central Washington. There, operators of big central-pivot sprinkler irrigation systems hoped they could make one 160-acre (64-hectare) circular sweep, washing the accumulating ash from their just emerging crops. In some cases it worked. In others, the plants folded over, permanently lodged in a wash of gray concretelike sludge.

Worse, however, was the discovery that the cover of ash was severely restricting infiltration: the absorption of irrigation water into the soil. Ponds quickly formed on the surface, then began draining away, while others sat and finally evaporated, leaving a hard, cracking surface.

As it turned out, the size of the ash particles—1 to 3 microns—allowed them to act as almost perfect plugs to fill the macropores in some soils, clogging them until they became almost impermeable. Farmers faced with this situation could only watch as their crops shriveled and died and hope that deep-tilling equipment would save the next year's crop by plowing the ash under.

Closer to the mountain, where the ash came down in even thicker blankets among shattered trees in the flattened forests, researchers quickly became aware they had real problems to cope with. Fred Swanson, at the US Forest Service's regional experiment station, soon realized that the rain and snow of the coming winter, com-

Far left:
Moving water erodes its way through the hard armorlike crust that formed atop the blanket of ash, quickly cutting deep gullies in the fresh debris deposits.

Left:
Spillway of new retaining structure put up by the US Army Corps of Engineers (left and right) is washed away, allowing floodwaters to pass unimpeded.

Right:
Hastily assembled army of men and machines works to gouge out the channel of the Cowlitz River, trying to enlarge a conduit able to accommodate the expected spring floods.

bined with the cover of light-weight, very loose ash, could create dangerously unmanageable problems. Along with other scientists from government agencies, universities, and timber companies, Swanson began surveying what the most likely short-term problems—and most costly long-term problems—might be. They found, for example, that the huge mudflows of May 18 had actually moved less than one tenth of 1 percent of the available dislodged material into the Cowlitz and Columbia river systems. But even that amount of sedimentation had stopped ship navigation, tying up the port of Portland, Oregon, at a cost of millions of dollars. It also cost millions to redredge a new shipping channel down the Columbia River.

It was already well known, of course, that nature responds quickly to catastrophic changes. Rainfall in June and early July quickly filled many depressions on the surface of the hummocky debris in the Toutle River valley, creating new lakes and ponds where the flow had blocked drainage. Streams that had once run cool and clear, well stocked with fish, were mostly jammed with tangled logs, forest debris, and ash and flowed with a sickly gray fluid.

On the mountain's slopes the erosional effects varied according to the composition of the ash and debris and the depth of deposits. To the northeast of the volcano, for example, thick layers of blast deposits had been followed by the arrival of pumice on July 22. A hard armored layer formed on the surface when the fine ash that gradually settled out of the air was wetted by summer rain and was

then dried quickly by the sun. This surface layer had the consistency of cold oatmeal before it dried. But when dry it was like hard plaster.

The numerous divots created when trees were uprooted by the May 18 blast were also filled with pumice, and as rains fell the water shed by the armored surface ran into the root-wad depressions, soaked into the ash deposits, and then ran beneath the surface crust through the porous layers below. In some places, where larger amounts of surface runoff began gathering and concentrating in preeruption gullies, enough erosive power was generated to cut through the plasterlike crust and rapidly excavate the pumice layer below, sometimes even floating blocks of pumice away.

As this rapid erosion continued, additional water that was flowing through the pumice layer combined with the surface waters to deepen and extend these gullies down through the new volcanic deposits, even down into the soil of the former forests. The initial result was the formation of deep but widely spaced gullies cutting into the steep, uneven slopes, mantled by the deep but water-resistant volcanic deposits.

For soil scientists, it is hard to imagine a more complex or less stable erosional situation.

In an effort to understand better what was going on, Swanson and his associates spent weeks driving hundreds of steel rods into the mountain's slopes, using them to carefully measure the thickness of the deposits and the depths of the

rills that formed between linear arrays of these erosion pins. Swanson hoped that by remeasuring these pins at the end of winter they might be able to determine how much material had been removed by erosion to be carried down the slopes and into stream channels.

On the northwest side of the mountain—where blast deposits had been directly covered by fine-textured volcanic ash—the rains of summer washed right over the waterproofed ash surface. On mountain slopes where lumbermen had harvested timber by clear-cutting before the eruption, the ash surface was smooth, punctuated only occasionally by random partially buried stumps. This pattern allowed surface waters to concentrate into rather evenly spaced rills that cut parallel tracks down the slopes. And since each of these smaller water courses tended to drain less surface area and carried less water, they did not develop sufficient erosive power to excavate below the preeruption surface. At the same, however, because they exposed the former soils to water and the sun's warmth, they triggered a virtual explosion of growth of fireweed and pearly everlasting, the first significant revegetation of this badly devastated area.

Below, in the former valleys of the Toutle and Muddy rivers, flowing water was trying to rebuild the drainage system that the debris flows and mud had obliterated. As the ponded waters that filled depressions in the debris flows began to overflow into other, lower depressions, the crude outlines of a new drainage pattern began to appear.

As this was occurring, and as it became obvious that the potential for erosion—and massive mudflows—was huge, the US Corps of Engineers and the US Geological Survey hastily prepared estimates of how much water and sediment might be disgorged from the St. Helens area through the coming winter. The US Soil Conservation Service also began the most massive aerial seeding operation in its history, hoping to retard some of the expected erosional effects by establishing vegetation where it could take root.

So while the Corps of Engineers and the Geological Survey were debating—the Army arguing that the Geological Survey's estimates were far too high, and the Survey arguing that the Army Engineers' plan to contain the flow of sediments was too skimpy to work—the Soil Conservation Service, using helicopters, was busily spreading large amounts of grass seed and fertilizer along critical erosional areas. And because of this work, a valuable lesson has been learned.

On the east side of Mount St. Helens, for instance, it was obvious that the helicopter-borne rotary spreaders were not applying the dry seed and powdery fertilizer very effectively. One could see that the tiny grass seeds did not go very far, while the dusty fertilizer seemed to blow away. And since the gray ash surface often reached high temperatures (65°C; 150°F) during August and September, it is not surprising that most of the seed broadcast over 8,100 hectares (20,000 acres) did not germinate, except in a few areas on streambanks.

To the west of the mountain, however, erosion control contractor Ed Marmolejo, from Estacada, Oregon, was using a different experimental approach called hydroseeding. This technique used a premixed recipe of seed, fertilizers, and a water-absorptive mulch, all put together with water in the rotating tub of a cement truck. While a helicopter waited, hovering, the cement truck disgorged a batch of the mixture into the aircraft's seeding bucket, and within a few seconds the helicopter was on its way to dump another load.

Marmolejo said, "It took us about four days to mobilize . . . but once we got started with our unique hopper loading system [the cement truck] we moved right along. You've heard of Yankee ingenuity? Well, I guess we're not exactly short of that stuff out here in the West."

Although Marmolejo's technique was more expensive than dry seeding, and the seed density is three times higher than with dry seeding, this approach created a 600-hectare (1,500-acre) green landmark in the middle of an otherwise desolate gray landscape.

Under normal conditions, floods that strike the Pacific Northwest usually occur as a result of warm rains, coming in from the ocean, falling upon deep snowpack that covers frozen, impermeable ground, often in the spring. In 1980, however, the critical moment came as a Christmas present in December. Late at night, on the 25th, warm rains moved in off the Pacific Ocean and began falling on light snowpack that covered the Mount St. Helens area. The snow, estimated at between 25 and 40 centimeters deep, quickly melted, loosing saturated slabs of ash to avalanche off steep hillsides. Tons of sediments and logs rushed down into the newly formed streambeds in the ash-covered valleys. Small depression ponds on the debris flows quickly overfilled, spilling their contents into the enlarging stream network. Streams that had been impounded by debris flows soon overflowed their new dams and in some cases burst through their confinements. Muddy rivers swelled along the flanks of the Toutle River debris flow, descending down the valley to attack the new sediment-catching structures that the US Corps of Engineers had just finished building.

This structure was not a dam, but merely a porous rock barrier designed to slow the flow of water sufficiently so as to let the highly erosive sediment settle out, keeping it from traveling downstream to block once more the Columbia River's ship channel. This $13 million rock barrier was almost 1.2 kilometers long and more than 11 meters high and was meant to be able to withstand twice the flow of any predicted 50-year flood.

But when the North Toutle River's flood waters crested about 9:30 A.M. on December 26, they were carrying away a huge load of logs and mud, as well as the spillway of the new retaining structure built by the Corps of Engineers. And, although less than 20 percent of the sediment trapped behind the structure was carried away by the floodwater, the downstream channels of the Toutle, Cowlitz, and Columbia rivers had to face the rest of winter unprotected, with little standing between them and the massive load of erodable material still waiting on the mountain's flanks and foothills. Already several sections of road that had survived the action of May 18 were wiped out by the rushing floodwater.

As the winter months continued, a massive $30 million project to dredge the channel of the Cowlitz River got underway in earnest. Large heaps of dredge spoil materials began lining the riverbanks as the Corps of Engineers' contractors worked to accommodate the large volume of water and sediments that were expected in the spring. Their main goal was to protect the towns of Castle Rock, Kelso, and Longview in Washington.

Fortunately, snow did come again to the Cascade Range, but not in its usual quantities. The skiers were disappointed but weather forecasters predicted—and got—mostly rain and little snow. Indeed, the amount of snow was so small that farmers living east of Mount St. Helens, who depend on spring and summer snowpack runoff for irrigation, began blaming the eruption for changing the climate. As March approached less than 25 percent of the normal water equivalent of snow had been deposited in the area.

After that Christmas flood, too, the Army's Corps of Engineers revised its flood forecast upward, but as the snowpack failed to build up, the Geological Survey began reducing its estimates. It became apparent that the feared Great Spring Flood of 1981 might not occur. And while some participants may want to claim credit for averting disaster by preparing for the floods, it was actually an unusually gentle winter that spared the Pacific Northwest yet another calamity—for awhile.

8 | *Later Eruptions and Dome Formation*

Perhaps it was too optimistic, but a lot of folks were hoping Mount St. Helens might settle down and let life return to normal once the massive eruptive blast of May 18, 1980, was over. Indeed, after that performance there seemed little more the volcano might do worth worrying about. Much of the lush green forest that once surrounded the volcano was gone, the beautiful rivers were jammed with mud and logs, and a choking, gritty blanket of gray ash had settled down on everything east.

But there was more to come. Only a week later, residents living west of the volcano in cities and towns such as Olympia, Vancouver, Longview, and Tacoma, Washington, began coping with a dusting of gray talcum-fine ash particles. They had pretty well escaped harm in the first, very massive eruption, but this time they experienced travails similar to those visited upon people living east of the mountain. Face masks were put into use, and automobiles began succumbing as the ash found its way into air cleaners and vital parts.

It was only seven days after the big blast, indeed, that Mount St. Helens let go with a second significant eruption, an explosive event that boosted ash clouds to 15 kilometers altitude and spread new ash flows down the cone's northern flank. Concurrently, winds above the mountain were blowing toward the northwest, west, and southwest, and as a result this fresh new column of ash was spread over a large area of southwestern Washington and northwestern Oregon.

As with the volcano's other eruptive episodes, this next event had been preceded—on May 24—by an increase in earthquake activity beneath the cone that was detected on the University of Washington's seismic array. Several hours later, the activity level decreased, and then, during early morning hours of May 25, the eruption began.

During this eruption apparently nobody was sufficiently close to the mountain to be hurt, but the renewal of activity, coming in the wake of the huge eruption of May 18, did serve notice that the mountain could not be taken for granted. It was obviously still alive, still active, still capable of dealing a deadly blow to the unwary and the unprepared.

Analysis of precursory earthquake activity beneath the mountain, supplemented by analysis of the gases emitted from the crater, gave seismologists, especially those at the University of Washington, reason to think that they could make rough predictions—and so be in a credible position to warn federal, state, and local safety officials—of impending eruptions, if not of their violence. Indeed, early seismic warning later did give officials time to pull ground crews out of the large red zone that had been established around the volcano.

On the evening of June 12, another large column of ash and steam came pouring from the breached crater. This activity peaked between 9 P.M. and midnight, generating a dark gray column that soared more than 7 miles (11 kilometers) high. Within two days, however, activity had again declined to the low level that had prevailed in the few preceding weeks. As a result of this June 12 eruption a load of ash came drifting toward the southwest, down on Vancouver, Washington, and Portland, Oregon, then westward toward Tillamook on the Oregon coast.

On June 13 observers reported a viscous lava dome had been extruded into Mount St. Helens's deeply breached crater. It had already grown to a diameter of 1,000 feet (300 meters) and piled up 130 feet (40 meters) high above the crater floor. This dome, a dark, broiling hot mound of cracked and broken lava, was surrounded by a light gray shelf of fine ash that had accumulated in the bottom of the crater. Steam could be seen jetting from fumaroles closer to the crater walls. The dome was described as a symmetrical circular mass colored tan to light gray. Its surface was cracked into a strange mosaic of polygonal blocks measuring from 15 to 35 feet (5 to 10 meters) across, resembling, geologists said, a large-scale bread-crust texture. They said the surfaces on the dome appeared to be only lightly covered with ash, while steam explosions were occurring at the northeast edge of the dome, kicking small amounts of ash into the air. Other fumarole zones were active almost all the way around the periphery of the new dome, and a small, shallow, irregular pond was seen in the southwest part of the crater. Damp ground in that area was greenish yellow, apparently a result of deposited sulfur.

Word that this June 12 eruption was about to begin had come from Prof. Steve Malone at the University of Washington, who

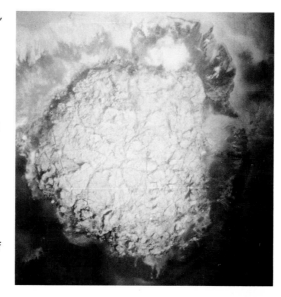

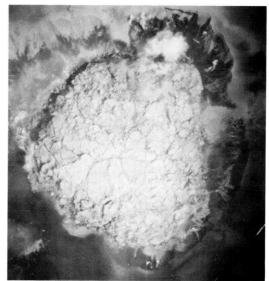

Vertical photo of the dacitic lava dome being extruded into the breached crater between June 12 and June 15.

noticed about 1 P.M. that he was beginning to see an increase in harmonic tremors beneath the mountain, plus small earthquake activity. He said the change didn't seem dramatic, but it was still the most significant change seen in the past few days.

Harmonic tremors arise from a continuous release of seismic energy, which contrasts sharply with the more sudden, distinct bursts of energy release associated with discrete earthquakes. It is believed that harmonic tremors are typically associated with the movement of magma underground.

Malone, in Seattle, contacted Don Mullineaux, chief US Geological Survey scientist, and Mullineaux in turn warned USGS field crews and local agencies that the change in activity was occurring. Later in the afternoon, too, Malone reported that the amplitude of the harmonic tremors had increased. Then, at 7:05 P.M., Malone saw a sharp increase in tremor amplitude and, at about the same time, radar observers at the airport in Portland, Oregon, reported an eruptive plume had soared to about 15,000 feet (4.6 kilometers) altitude. Unfortunately, poor visibility prevents observations from the ground, but it was generally concluded that the harmonic tremor activity and eruption of the tall plume coincided.

Malone reported that the tremor continued at high level until about 8 P.M., then declined abruptly to a low level. This pattern, he said, was similar to what had occurred in association with the May 25 eruption. Then, at 9:11 P.M., a dramatic increase in harmonic tremor activity was detected. And from the field, from a US Forest Service spotter plane, observers reported another eruptive plume had risen to at least 36,000 feet (11 kilometers), while the Portland airport's radar observers said it reached altitudes close to 50,000 feet (16 kilometers).

After that event, activity remained vigorous until about midnight, when the recordings of harmonic tremors—and the height of the eruptive plume—began to decline. Malone reported that during all these eruptions harmonic tremor was observed, and that it gradually died away over a period of several hours as the eruption lost strength.

Side-looking airborne radar (SLAR) image of the deep crater of Mount St. Helens during the eruption of June 12, 1980. Note the three distinct eruption vents.

Despite the violence of this activity, hydrologists at the scene reported no new flows down the Toutle River. Ash from the eruption generally drifted southwest from the volcano, and a few pyroclastic flows did come down the north slope of Mount St. Helens toward Spirit Lake. Temperatures measured in these new ash flows were startling, since they exceeded any that had been measured in deposits laid down by the May 18 eruption. The material deposited included dense, dark gray pumice and some tan vesicular pumice.

Once the dome was in place, the volcano seemed to settle down, and it was more than a month before the next event, a major explosive eruption, sent a large column of steam and ash boiling into the sky. Preceding this activity, which came in three bursts or pulses, seismologists had recorded 14 small, shallow earthquakes similar in character to the temblors that were detected just prior to the huge eruption of May 18. Activity then increased, with 32 more earthquakes being recorded, and then the eruption occurred, producing a seismic signal that lasted for 250 seconds. The second eruption pulse produced seismic signals lasting 450 seconds, and the third episode produced harmonic tremors lasting for almost an hour.

The first ash eruption in this episode lasted only 6 minutes, but the eruptive cloud of ash and steam rose to almost 50,000 feet (14 kilometers) before being carried off to the northeast by high-altitude winds. The second eruption followed at 6:25 P.M., lasting 22 minutes, sending a plume of hot ash and steam to an altitude of 55,000 feet (18 kilometers). The third, and longest, eruption of July 22 came at 7:01 P.M. and lasted for 2 hours. The main ash cloud was blown to the northeast, and satellite photos showed that it traveled northeast, apparently crossing into Canada near the Washington-Idaho border. Also during this series of eruptions, pyroclastic flows of ash, gas, and steam were reported streaming down the north flank of the mountain.

As this was going on, Charles Rosenfeld and Chief Warrant Officer George Burns, of the Oregon National Guard, were aboard a powerful Mohawk aircraft surveying the activity in the crater. Rosenfeld recalled the incident as follows:

Surface of the pumice flows, which had descended into the Toutle River valley through the gap in the north wall of the crater. The pumice blocks range from 1 inch to 7 feet (2 centimeters to 2 meters) in diameter.

Below:
After the June eruption, the new dacitic dome attained a diameter of almost 1,165 feet (350 meters) and a height of more than 130 feet (40 meters).

Right:
Series of brief glimpses made in June confirming that the dome was growing, with the fractured bread-crust texture of the dome surface showing signs of expansion.

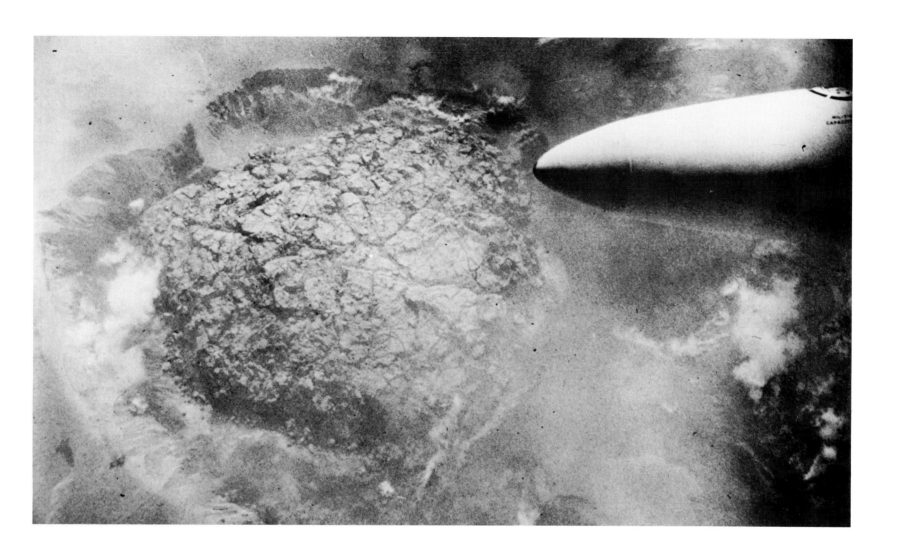

We opted to make a vertical pass only 3,000 feet above, and directly over, the shattered remnants of the June dome, hoping to acquire a thermal infrared image during the lull immediately following the eruption. At 9:08 P.M., as we passed northward, over the precipitous south wall of the crater, a fourth—but, fortunately, smaller—burst occurred from a large north/south trending trench that bisected the former dome.

As Burns nimbly banked the Mohawk, getting us over the crater rim to the west, I was able to observe and photograph the plume as it first spewed out to fill the crater. We saw the burst first shoot out laterally from the trench; then it quickly boiled upward to about 4,000 meters above the crater.

Other observers in helicopters and fixed-wing aircraft also got good views of what was going on. In a preliminary, unofficial US Geological Survey report on the action, geologist Rick Hoblitt reported from his log,

Flying from east to west approximately one mile north of the vent. Following a period of a few seconds duration, during which rate of gas release increases, an "ash fountain" is ejected to about 1500 feet above the vent; as the projections of the fountain arc over and reach the surface in the vicinity of the vent, they give rise to a pyroclastic flow that begins to rapidly flow northward out of the amphitheater. We exit to the west as quickly as possible.

Hoblitt then notes, "We land at toe of a flow lobe to quickly take a temperature reading. Maximum reading 685°C at about 10 centimeters [depth], lower temperatures at greater depths."

The scene was described similarly by geologist Harry Glicken, also in a helicopter, who noted from his log, "Beginning of major ash emission from dome site observed. Instead of rising vertically, light gray cloud of ash fills width of amphitheater [crater] in less than one second and heads north, hugging ground surface. Helicopter begins to head west at tremendous speed."

It became evident during this eruption that the large lava dome that had been extruded into the base of the crater after the June 12 eruption was being broken up and carried away. An observer in another airplane, Jim Vallance, reported that the behavior of the ash plumes "could perhaps be attributed to removal of the remaining dome during the second pulse." He added that "it seemed to me that pyroclastic flows of both the second and third pulses boiled out of the vent and behaved fluidly much like soup."

Later, Hoblitt and Norman Banks visited the mountain to examine the materials from the pyroclastic flows and reported that two new layers of material were visible on top of the earlier deposits. Of these two flows, "the lower unit is cream-colored, while the upper unit has a faint pink/salmon color. The thickness of these flows averages one to two meters." They also reported that temperature measurements—taken at three locations one day after the deposits were emplaced—produced readings of 608°F (320°C) at 22 inches (55 centimeters) depth, 1252°F (678°C) at 40 inches (100 centimeters) depth, and 1,301°F (705°C) at 60 inches (150 centimeters) depth.

It was after this July 22 eruption that data on gas flow from Mount St. Helens were found to probably be useful for predicting future eruptions. It was noted that after the explosive event the amount of carbon dioxide issuing from the crater was high, while the flow of sulfur dioxide was low. Two days later, however, sulfur dioxide emissions returned to their former high level, stayed there until the end of the month, and then decreased abruptly, twofold. The carbon dioxide emissions remained high.

At that point, July 29, a prediction of an eruption on or about August 6 was made. Geologist Don Harris said that the prediction was based on the reduced flow of sulfur dioxide emissions during the period from July 5 to July 22, a deficit amounting to something like 15,000 tons per day. He explained,

The working hypothesis is that the magmatic gas emissions decreased prior to eruptions because of decreases in the permeability of the material in the margins of the partially sealed magma body. The deficit in gas emissions preceding the July 22 eruption is quantitatively related (not necessarily equal) to the production rate of gas at depth in the magma body.

This suggests that with time a magma body's periphery gradually becomes impermeable to the flow of carbon dioxide and sulfur dioxide, and as it approaches the point of eruption the flow of these gases drops off markedly. This, indeed, is what happened in late July and early August, just before a relatively small eruption occurred on August 7, which was followed by emplacement of a new dacitic dome in the crater.

Harris observed a "decrease by a factor of four [in the flow of carbon dioxide] between August 3 and August 6. At 12:33 A.M. on August 7, the scientist in charge was notified of the significant change in carbon dioxide emission and that an eruption was likely within a short period of time." The eruption came late that afternoon, Thursday, August 7.

Based on this work, Harris suggested that "the occurrence of large gas-rich puffs from the crater of the volcano before and after eruptions may indicate transitions between the well sealed and poorly sealed states characterized by the gas emission variations."

Two other workers interested in gas flow from the volcano—W. I. Rose and T. J. Bornhorst, from Michigan—noted that the passive flux of gas coming from Mount St. Helens tended to be high compared to the flow of sulfur dioxide from other fuming volcanoes. This, they said, suggests that a significant body of magma might have been lodged close to the surface beneath the mountain. They added that

an overall increase in sulfur dioxide flux rates measured from May 18 to early July may reflect the ascent and equilibration of this dacitic magma.

The mildly decreasing trend measured since July could be due to the solidification and sealing of the border of that magma body, a process that is periodically interrupted by fracturing and degassing events.

During these degassing events, sulfur dioxide, which presumably is less soluble, tends to be released prior to carbon dioxide. . . . This has important implications for forecasting. The wide separation of sulfur dioxide and carbon dioxide peaks in event two suggests that new magma may have been emplaced from depth at that time. Newly decompressed magma might reflect best the different solubilities of the two gases.

The period July 5 to 20 was [also] marked by seismic activity which could have been associated with new magma introduction.

As with these earlier eruptions, the event on August 7 was also preceded by volcanic tremors. Unlike the others, however, the August 7 eruption was not preceded by a decrease in tremor amplitude. The tremors appeared to come in distinct bursts lasting 10 to 20 seconds that were randomly spaced in time. Then, at

Photograph of the fourth eruption plume, July 22, 1980. The aircraft was about half a mile (1 kilometer) above the crater when the photo was taken.

4:27 P.M., a large seismic event was recorded that apparently marked the beginning of the eruption.

Prior to this eruption, the volcano had settled into a relatively quiet condition, even though the crater area was still fuming, sending columns of condensing water vapor to elevations of perhaps 12,000 feet (3,500 meters). A reddish glow was usually visible within the vent crater as daylight waned.

Rosenfeld noted, however, that "the ashfall from this [August 7] eruption was light, so I was able to fly to the northwest flank of the mountain even during the eruption."

The first burst from that eruption produced a plume that rose to about 8 miles (13.5 kilometers) altitude, and it was easily measured by radar at the airport in Portland, Oregon. At the same time, a small pumice-rich ashflow sped across the flank of the mountain below the breached northern side of the crater, reaching part of the way to Spirit Lake while leaving a thin deposit along its course. A series of smaller bursts of eruptive activity followed, and the sequence was ended with a terminating burst, nearly as large as the first, at about 10:30 P.M. As this occurred, the intensity of the volcanic tremors began decreasing, and they were followed by a series of rather deep earthquakes.

On the following morning, August 8, a new dome began pushing its way up through the crater floor, half filling the vent crater by the end of the day. It had filled the smaller crater by August 10, when it stopped growing. For the balance of the month, the volcano remained essentially quiet, providing very few earthquakes and no eruptions. Observers did note continuing incandescence in the walls of the vent crater, plus some large cracks in the surface of the newly emplaced lava dome. Gas emissions continued fluctuating between moderate and low levels.

At the same time, on the flanks of the volcano, drainage patterns that had been blocked or changed by the fall of debris and ash were gradually being reestablished. The restoration of flow included new channels being cut across what was described as "the hummocky surface" of the debris flow that had buried the North Toutle River's valley.

In the last two weeks of August water from Maratta Creek—which had been impounded by a new levee made up of debris flow materials—suddenly let go, releasing a large flow of water that poured down across the debris flow and formed a pond in a small depression, just a few kilometers above Camp Baker. This pond was estimated to be holding some 370,000 cubic yards (290,000 cubic meters) of water. On August 27, however, the pond water washed over the rim, cut itself a deep outlet and cascaded down into a check dam constructed by the US Corps of Engineers. A large amount of this water remained behind the dam, but enough poured over to damage construction equipment and destroy a few temporary bridges and access roads. Varying amounts of damage were inflicted all the way down to the town of Toutle.

One team of researchers, Banks and Hoblitt, made numerous and repeated measurements of the debris flow materials during August. They found, even 86 days after the May 18 eruption, that 32 feet (10 meters) deep into the pyroclastic flow the temperatures had dropped only 35 to 55°F (20 to 30°C) from the time the flows had been emplaced. Thinner deposits, those between 6 and 10 feet (2 and 3 meters) thick, had cooled to only about a third from their original temperatures at the time of emplacement.

Other efforts were made to determine temperatures inside the crater, even on the dacitic dome itself. Banks and Hoblitt noted that "several attempts were made with the aerial penetrator and temperature-sensitive paints to assess the surface temperatures in the vent crater and temperatures in glowing cracks in the post-August 7 dome, and in the remaining walls of the June dome."

The results of this work were mixed. But they did indicate local surface temperatures—within the moat surrounding the dome—ranged between 212 and 660°F (100 and 350°C) and that some of the glowing cracks in the dome itself were as hot as 1,200°F (650°C). As a result, they warned, "these temperatures, in addition to other physical problems [such as 300-foot- (100-meter-) high northern cliffs and glowing rock piles in the south], indicate that attempts to sample the dome or the crater gases, or to measure crater temperatures, would best be done by remote control."

Thermograph images show that heat permeates the entire dome. High-temperature sensors indicated that the extreme heat [more than 900°F (500°C)] was most easily detected along the fractures in the expanding surface. (Oregon Army National Guard image)

Rosenfeld also noted that his thermal infrared images, acquired during an Oregon National Guard surveillance flight using a Mohawk aircraft, showed that the remnants of the June dome were still cooling in the walls of the moat around the new, smaller August dome. In addition, apparently more heat was beginning to emanate from a series of fractures that were seen to be radiating away from the dome, like spokes of a wheel.

During most of September the volcano was essentially quiet, and poor weather hampered observations of the dome, the amphitheaterlike crater, and surrounding areas. But in October, Mount St. Helens began performing in earnest again, producing its sixth and longest eruption, which included a sequence of five major emissions accompanied by at least two pyroclastic flows.

Prior to this activity, field observers had noted prominent cracks forming on the crater floor and near the crest of the rampart. When first noticed in mid-September, these cracks were concentrated mostly toward the northern side of the crater, were several centimeters wide, and tended to radiate away from the dome. Measurements showed that the cracks gradually widened through the rest of the month and into October. Also, as measurements were continued, many new cracks were noticed on September 23, and they began widening in the next several days. These widening cracks were emitting fumes, and those on the northeast side of the crater were seen to be glowing bright orange. Temperatures, measured at a depth of about 1.5 meters, were recorded at 1,328 to 1,540°F (720 to 838°C).

Geologist Don Swanson from the US Geological Survey, Menlo Park, California, suggested that this new cracking activity on the crater floor before the long October eruption could have occurred in response to either the rise of a new magma body within the cone or the cooling effect of heavy rainfall. Rain gauges on the mountain did indicate that rainfall had been substantial during a period of several days before the October eruption. After that eruption, Swanson reported, new cracks were noticed and efforts were being made to keep a record of their activity.

New bursts of activity began about October 7, when increased gas emissions, some carrying ash into the sky, were observed. The incandescent cracks were also seen, and the seismic record included low-level tremors and shallow local earthquakes. Then, on October 16, the mountain began a long eruption sequence, starting with a major plume event at 9:58 P.M. Just before the plume came boiling out of the crater, a US Forest Service observer reported seeing a strong incandescent glow within the crater. The ash plume from this eruption soared to 40,000 feet (12,800 meters) altitude, and winds from the northwest carried the ash generally to the south, into northern Oregon.

The next day, a second major eruptive event began at 9:28 A.M., sending an ash plume even higher, to 47,000 feet (14,300 meters) altitude. During this eruption a video camera—which had been installed on the new feature named Harry's Ridge—spotted the beginning of a new pyroclastic flow, which apparently came out of the western side of the breached crater, flowing down toward the base of the feature now known as The Steps.

Then, shortly after noon on October 17, field observers reported that the dome, which had been built after the August 7 eruption, was gone.

Eruptions continued sending plumes of ash and gas into the air on October 17 and 18, and at 2:28 P.M. on the 18th the final blast of this series was recorded. Within an hour, field observations of the floor of the crater became possible. It was seen to have become a broad, shallow depression, and a small new dome had been put in place.

As the volcano continued to quiet down, however, observers could see the new dome growing. Swanson reported,

The dome was emplaced rapidly, but required several days to adjust to its new status. It began to grow within a shallow depression indenting the floor of a 250–300-meter-diameter crater directly south of the rampart.

The dome was first observed at 1520 [3:20 P.M.] October 18, about 45 minutes after the end of the eruption, when it was estimated [to be] 5 meters high and 25 meters wide. An hour later it had grown to an estimated 10 meters high and 40 meters across, and deep glowing cracks scored the crust of the blocky mass. At 1830 [6:30 P.M.] guesses put it at 20 to 25 meters high and 50 to 70 meters wide.

By this time, the dome filled the shallow depression, spread a short distance onto the floor of the crater, and stood higher than most of the rampart. Large slabs were breaking off the steep—in places overhanging—sides of the dome, crashing to the crater floor and breaking up. Small trickles of orange-red viscous lava oozed from points on the west and particularly east sides; the eastern stream fed a small pond in the moat between the dome and the crater wall. An orange flame flickered from several holes in the side of the dome.

By October 19, Swanson reported, this new dome had covered most of the crater floor, reaching a diameter of about 600 feet (185 meters) and a height of about 170 feet (50 meters). The dome's surface was cut by deep cracks that showed glowing, incandescent walls. In addition, several spires were seen that reached a few meters above the dome's surface. Indeed, Swanson said that "to one hungry observer, the dome resembled the top of a gigantic bran muffin fresh from the oven."

Unlike the earlier domes, however, this new October dome, as it began cooling, changed shape rather dramatically. It subsided by about 60 feet (18 meters) and widened by some 50 feet (15 meters). A small depression formed near the dome's center, and large cracks, some as deep as 25 feet (7 meters), radiated from the depressed center roughly toward the four points of the compass.

Swanson suggested that this behavior of the extruding dome meant it was perhaps

formed by magma less viscous and with smaller yield strength than that of the [larger] June dome. One way to produce these differences is to assume that the October magma was hotter than the June magma. Interestingly, small inclusions of vesicular basalt, although uncommon, occur more frequently in the October dome and earlier pumice than in older 1980 pumice. . . . The presence of such inclusions raises the possibility of magma mixing, a way to reduce the viscosity of the dominant silicic component both by raising its temperature and by slight chemical mixing with more fluid basaltic magma.

Teams working in the field found that by October 22 the dome had cooled sufficiently so that they could do some sampling. As Swanson reported it, the only difficulties encountered were related to the large amount of heat and gas being emitted through cracks in the new tephra deposits found on the inner walls of the crater. The sampled part of the dome was found to have a scoriaceous rather than bread-crusted texture, and was apparently more crystalline than the pumice ejected earlier in the eruption.

Interesting results were also obtained from crews who had been watching for deformation of the mountain and its features. In September and October, before the long eruption sequence began, measurements of the field stations indicated the mountain was swelling slightly, especially on the north side beneath the rampart near the breached crater. Observers noted that much of this deformational change appeared to be correlated with the rather vigorous release of gases from the volcano. In September, for example, field crews who occupied geodetic sites found evidence for slow expansion of the mountain. On September 24, however, a strong discharge of gas came from the crater, and scientists who occupied the geodetic network a few days later found that the mountain had contracted slightly.

During the eruption sequence in October, however, instruments and observation posts set up for the geodetic network did not fare very well. One station, called Deep Throat, set up on September 17, was found in terrible condition after the October eruption: bent, charred, and its prism gone. It was soon reestablished, however, as Deep Throat II. Another station, called Delta, consisted of an 800-pound steel tower that had been erected by the Portland Power and Light Company. In the October 16 ashflow, Delta was shoved 1,200 feet (375 meters) downslope, apparently cartwheeling and losing its neck before coming to a stop. The damaged tower was renamed Wreckage, and a new reflector was attached to its high point so that it could be used in further geodetic survey work.

The work, of course, continued, and in November the volcano exhibited the relatively benign behavior similar to what had occurred in September. The geodetic network detected continued swelling of the volcano, especially on its north flank, and seismic activity also continued, but at a relatively low level. The most interesting seismic event came on November 17, when a harmonic tremor lasting a full 9 minutes was recorded on the University of Washington's seismic network. On November 22 a new fumarole opened up on the southeast side of the dome in the crater, and more venting was also seen on the northeast side of the dome.

One of these new fumaroles, located slightly east of an old main fumarole sampled earlier, appeared to be making more noise than any fumarole previously examined, sounding much like a very loud jet engine. Both this fumarole and the southeast fumarole were seen emitting puffs of gas at rather regular half-second intervals, and the walls of both vents were seen glowing dull red.

Weather conditions also worsened for the observers. Instruments became lined with rime ice, below freezing temperatures were common, and strong east winds made work on the mountain difficult. Fortunately, however, only two storms carrying significant amounts of snow hit the area, and much of the snow that did fall was rather quickly blown off the bare mountain slopes. It became difficult to reach some instrument stations, however, and field workers said use of snowshoes did help in some instances.

On November 5 and 6 a major rainstorm deposited enough water in the crater to create a rather large lake in an area known as the Pumice Pond. On the second day of the rainstorm, the lake covered about one fourth of the crater floor. Swanson also noted that "the lake merges imperceptibly into 'dry' land; the transition zone is extremely treacherous, as it is little more than floating pumice and ash. Seepage of the lake water into the still hot June 12 ashflow generated small phreatic [steam] explosions and bubbling mudpots."

As for the dome, it was obviously cooling even in early November. It changed very little, and by November 12 snow was beginning to stick on its cooler areas. At the same time, between November 12 and November 18, a small pond formed in the eastern part of the crater at the bottom of a big talus pile. As best as could be determined, however, this pond soon disappeared.

As December arrived, activity in the crater began accelerating once again, and observers felt that the changes were pointing rather obviously to another eruptive episode, which did finally arrive in January 1981. By mid-December, for example, noticeable changes had occurred around the edges of the new dome that had been emplaced in October. Ground parties visiting the crater reported that the fumaroles were turning on and off in different areas—like a pipe organ—at the periphery of the dome. On December 12, observers noted that the southeast side of the

Left:
Photograph of the growing October dome.

Right:
Photograph of the Muffie dome.

dome apparently was fuming more than had been reported earlier. Indeed, a day later the size of the plume from the southeast side of the dome had increased markedly, and scientists surmised that a local lateral blast had blown a triangular wedge out of the side of the dome toward the southeast, in such a way that the debris from the blast remained inside the crater. At the same time, large cracks in the ground were observed and, as monitoring continued, they were seen to widen and grow longer.

Between December 25 and December 28, cloudy weather obscured the view into the crater. On the 28th, however, observers from the Forest Service and the Geological Survey could view the crater from a light plane. What they saw was a new extrusion of lava measuring some 165 feet (50 meters) in diameter that had grown as tall as the existing dome. This new eruptive feature was pushing its way up through the southeast quadrant of the existing dome, and by the end of the month it stood some 250 feet (75 meters) taller than the October dome.

As this newer part of the dome continued its growth, the crater floor began deforming dramatically, creating new thrust faults and some uplifted zones to the northeast, south, and southwest of the dome. Cracks in the crater floor were also growing faster, and geodetic data indicated that the northeast rampart was being moved significantly.

On another side of the dome, on the northwest, a second auxiliary lobe began squeezing itself out next to the main dome, creating another extension to what had become a multilobe composite dome occupying the crater floor of Mount St. Helens.

In Swanson and his colleagues' interpretation of these events, the northward movement of the rampart was probably a result of increasing pressure from volatiles trapped in a shallow magma reservoir system. Increased activity of fumaroles during the October-to-December period released enough gas pressure to avoid a large eruption, they reasoned, but once this activity ceased—perhaps because of new magma sealing off the escape vents—the pressure increased again, permitting fresh magma to be lifted up toward the surface. According to this scenario, the fumaroles may have acted as safety valves.

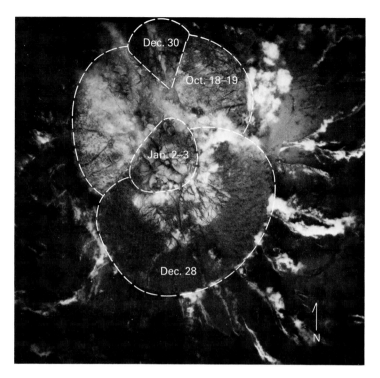

Vertical view of the December–January composite dome.

In a summary of December's activity, Swanson said that several things seemed clear. First, the crater's floor was being changed, becoming both distended and cracked. Also, the dome itself apparently was becoming unstable, as evidenced by the blowout on the southeast side and the emissions of plumes. Moreover, fumarole activity seemed to be declining, hinting that some sort of sealing process was under way that might begin trapping the volatiles again. And temperatures apparently were rising, as shown by an increasing number of cracks that were glowing orange red with heat, and by the shallow depth of this glow.

"It is really no wonder that we were expecting some major event to transpire," Swanson said, "and it did. The eruption may have begun in late December, but the magma for that eruption was rising detectably for at least two weeks before."

Technical Vignette: Harmonic tremor
Michael Fehler

Seismometers located near volcanoes have recorded two distinct types of ground motion. One type of motion is similar in nature to those recorded during earthquakes that occur in many places throughout the world. The second type of motion is recorded only near active volcanoes and has been given the name volcanic or harmonic tremor. There are seismograms of typical earthquakes and harmonic tremors recorded by seismometers placed near Mount St. Helens. The typical earthquake seismogram shows definite change in character with time. The initial high-frequency portion of the trace is a representation of the ground motion caused by body waves traveling through the rock between the earthquake and the seismometer. The later part of the trace, which consists of waves of lower frequency, represents surface waves that travel along the surface of the earth between the earthquake and the seismometer. The typical harmonic-tremor seismogram consists of a trace that shows almost no change in frequency with time. Seismologists have been unable to identify arrivals of different types of waves such as body or surface waves on seismograms of harmonic tremor.

We now know that earthquakes are caused by motion of the earth in opposite directions across two sides of a fault. Seismologists currently have no simple explanation for harmonic tremor. Much evidence exists for associating harmonic tremor with movement of magmas through the plumbing system beneath a volcano. Measurements on the Kilauea volcano in Hawaii indicate that the summit of the volcano often deflates or decreases in elevation just prior to the occurrence of harmonic tremor. This deflation is considered to be caused by movement of magma out along one of the rift zones of the volcano from a magma reservoir located beneath the summit of the mountain. These rift zones are the sites of major eruptions of Kilauea. By measuring the amplitude of ground motion at various places along the rift zone, seismologists can infer that the region where disturbances within the volcano are generating harmonic tremor is moving progressively farther out along the rift zone with time. The disturbed region continues to progress out along the rift zone until an eruption occurs.

Various models to explain harmonic tremor have been proposed. According to one of these models, harmonic tremor is caused not by a shearing motion along a fracture in the earth, as is the case with earthquakes, but by the fracturing of rock due to forceful intrusion of magma. Other seismologists believe that harmonic tremor is caused by a resonance effect in the magma conduit similar to what occurs in a pipe organ. Still other scientists believe that harmonic tremor is due to resonance of the magma chamber beneath the volcano where magma accumulates prior to an eruption.

One further piece of information on this matter is the observation that at Mount St. Helens harmonic tremor occurs prior to eruptions when there is no dome present at the summit of the volcano. When a dome is present, no harmonic tremor occurs prior to eruption.

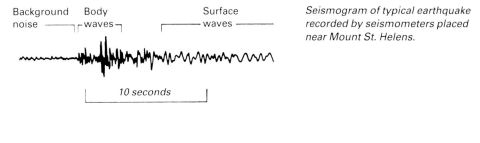

Background noise — Body waves — Surface waves

10 seconds

Seismogram of typical earthquake recorded by seismometers placed near Mount St. Helens.

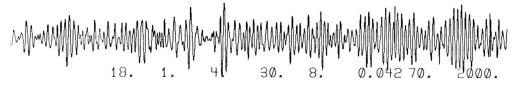

18.   1.   4   30.   8.   0.042 70.   2000.

22.5 SEC.

Seismogram of typical harmonic tremors recorded by seismometers placed near Mount St. Helens.

Technical Vignette:
The volcanic domes
Charles Rosenfeld

Given experience with other similar stratovolcanoes, geologists suspected it would not be long before Mount St. Helens would begin extruding a thick, pasty form of dacitic lava that would form into a vent-choking volcanic dome.

Formation of the dome began after the large eruption of June 12, which had sent pumice flows cascading down from the summit crater, down the northern flank to overtop the flows released by the eruption of May 25. At the time, the summit crater was hidden by a dense blanket of clouds.

Then, on June 15, when the skies cleared and observation became possible, a US Forest Service officer, in a light plane, caught the first glimpse of the lava dome forming within the breached crater. The new dome was light gray and estimated to be 200 meters in diameter and perhaps 40 meters high, exhibiting what was referred to as a cracked bread-crust surface.

Growth of the dome was monitored through the second half of the month, although cloudiness, steam, and airborne ash generally frustrated attempts to measure it accurately. The viscous lava dome obviously did grow, however, reaching a diameter of 350 meters and a height of over 45 meters by June 20.

On July 22, however, following intensifying seismic activity, a major explosive eruption began at 5:14 P.M. (Pacific Daylight Time), followed by two successive blasts at 6:30 P.M. and 7:02 P.M., which deposited new pumaceous flows atop the earlier flows. This powerful eruption resulted in burial and partial destruction of the June dome and created a keyhole-shaped trench containing a small crater. Volcanic bombs of cracked lava, presumably fragmented remains of the June dome, were collected for study by crews in helicopters and were identified lithologically as dacite.

On August 7, more seismic signals—harmonic tremors—heralded an ash-rich volcanic eruption that began at 4:25 P.M., opening a deep crater that perforated the remains of the broken June dome. During the next three days a new dacitic dome began forming over the vent as fresh viscous lava was extruded from below. It grew until almost reaching above the rim of the crater, attaining a maximum diameter of 200 meters by August 20. Portions of this new dacite dome were seen to be glowing all through the month of September.

This relatively small August dome disappeared abruptly, however, when an eruptive period began on October 16. This event produced at least five major blasts and two extensive pyroclastic flows. Then a new dacitic dome began to form, replacing the August dome, growing at a dramatic rate on October 18 and 19.

This new dome, called the October dome, was first seen at 3:20 P.M. (about 45 minutes after the end of the eruption on October 18), at which time it was only 10 meters in diameter and only 5 meters high. But an hour later it had grown to a height of 10 meters and was 40 meters across. As it continued this rapid rate of growth, the new dome began to spread across the crater floor, and by nightfall large slabs of lava were seen breaking off the steep sides of the dome. This allowed orange-red viscous lava to ooze out onto the floor of the crater, and orange flames were seen flickering from several points along the flanks of the dome.

Observers who saw the dome on the morning of October 19 reported it had grown to almost 185 meters in diameter and had reached a height of 50 meters. It was nicknamed Muffie because of its resemblance to a large steaming bran muffin just removed from the oven. But then the large dome partially collapsed like a soufflé before October 29, subsiding by about 18 meters and expanding outward nearly 15 meters at its base.

Geologists said it was reasonable to assume that collapse of the dome signaled the end of magma extrusion from the subterranean chamber and stagnation of the magma in the volcano's vent, thereby allowing the viscous magma inside the dome to sag under its own weight.

In comparing the October dome Muffie with the first dome extruded in June, it should be remembered that the June dome had three or four times the volume of Muffie and that it was extruded into place over an 8-day period without sagging or collapsing. It seems, then, that Muffie may have been hotter, and perhaps less viscous, allowing for faster extrusion and subsequent deformation.

But Muffie did not last very long either. On December 13, a lateral blast from the vent blew a triangular 60-meter-wide wedge out of the dome toward the southeastern wall of the crater. Large dense blocks of dacite were displaced by this blast, and the largest, nearly

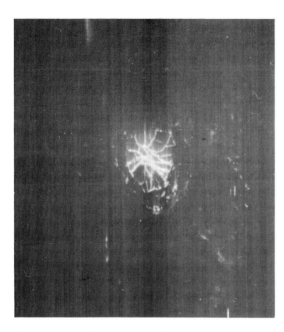

Thermograph showing expansion cracks (greater than 600°C) during growth of the June dome.

10 meters in diameter, was moved at least 40 meters by the explosion. The walls in the blowout zone appeared to be relatively dense rock, contrasting with the scoriaceous crust of the dome itself.

As the new year approached, a new 50-meter-diameter dome started being extruded toward the southeast through the blast area in the Muffie dome, while a second, smaller extrusive dome appeared at the northwest edge of the dome.

On January 2 and 3, however, the new southeast dome—which had been growing quite slowly—began to inflate rapidly, eventually reaching a height of about 100 meters. As this was occurring, another dome began extruding up through the center of the October dome, up through Muffie, eventually completely covering the former dome and growing to nearly 70 meters by January 5, when it suddenly began to collapse. In this process it lost perhaps 10 meters of its height, suggesting that the magma being extruded was becoming quite fluid.

Harmonic tremors—which have become a relatively reliable seismic precursor of activity at Mount St. Helens—intensified on February 4 and then began to diminish. This seismic activity was herald of the extrusion of the largest, most rapidly growing dome yet produced, and scientists quickly nicknamed it Dome-zilla.

From February 5 to February 7, Dome-zilla grew until it covered most of the central and December domes and most of the eastern flank of the whole dome complex, leaving only the southeastern December dome exposed to view. By the evening of February 7, Dome-zilla had attained a height of 135 meters, and the next morning began at least a partial collapse.

Given this type of activity, prolonged over many months, it appeared that the volcano was setting itself up for multiple, repeated extrusions of dome material and for the growth of a complex plug dome. These late eruptions were not as heavily charged with gases and were not so explosive, perhaps indicating that a trend toward extrusion of more fluid lavas was developing. In addition, rather than removing the old dome explosively, as had happened to the first few domes, later activity merely extruded more fluid lava around the former dome or through places where the earlier dome had begun to collapse. This suggested that they may be sharing a common magma conduit.

9 | Lessons and Questions

The tall dark plume of ash, steam, and gas boiling up from the shattered cone of Mount St. Helens stood tall on the horizon as the high-flying U-2 spy plane arrived on the scene from California. The single-seat observation plane, dispatched from the National Aeronautics and Space Administration's Ames Research Center, was gathering samples of gas and dust in the stratosphere, measuring what the volcano was injecting into the earth's atmospheric circulation system.

The U-2, of course, is famous as the once secret spy plane that was shot down in 1956 over the Soviet Union with pilot Gary Powers at the controls. For the Mount St. Helens work, however, it and several other exotic craft had been fitted with seven experiments designed by scientists involved in NASA's Aerosol Climatic Effects (ACE) program at Ames. Their goal was to measure what aerosols, of what size and what chemistry were being carried high into the stratosphere above the volcano.

But the experiments carried aboard the U-2 were only a small part of the work done in the air and on the ground to study the volcanic eruption. Indeed, the Mount St. Helens eruption was turning out to be the most thoroughly studied, best-documented volcanic event in history. Squads of scientists—using helicopters, airplanes, four-wheel-drive vehicles and long-range observing instruments—descended on southwestern Washington to set up shop and learn what they could about the mountain and its activities.

Seismologists, for example, were able to record a whole series of underground events that started with small earthquakes, developed into earthquake swarms, and then became harmonic tremors as magma moved into the mountain. Even as the mountain's seismic activity was accelerating, teams of field geologists were surrounding it with an array of new and sensitive seismometers. Thus, within months, as the eruptions continued, a team of seismologists at the University of Washington, in Seattle, became able to predict eruptions—even to within a few hours.

At the same time, other scientists were setting up infrared instruments around the steaming volcanic cone, taking readings on the mountain's changing heat patterns. These observations, however, did not prove to be as useful for making predictions. But

Right:
Computer-enhanced thermal infrared image—or thermograph—of Mount St. Helens just a day before the massive eruption of May 18, 1980. In the crater area, to the right, can be seen two thermal anomalies corresponding to the craters that formed during eruptive activity in March. Also visible are scattered hot spots throughout what was the dangerous bulge area. (Oregon Army National Guard image)

Below:
Computer-enhanced thermal infrared image taken at 5:52 A.M. on May 18, the day of the huge, cataclysmic eruption. The patterns of thermal activity appear to be the same as those seen in earlier thermographs, with no major new activity evident. Nonetheless, the massive eruption occurred only 2.5 hours later. (Oregon Army National Guard image. Digital enhancement by Geography Department, Oregon State University)

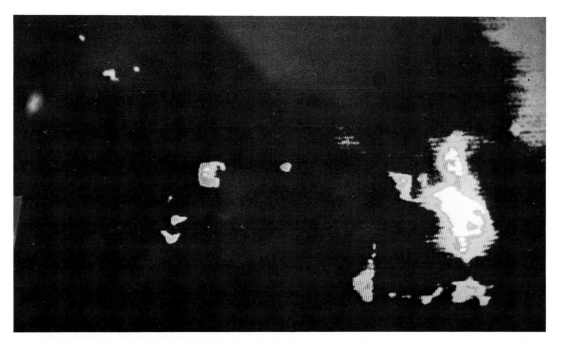

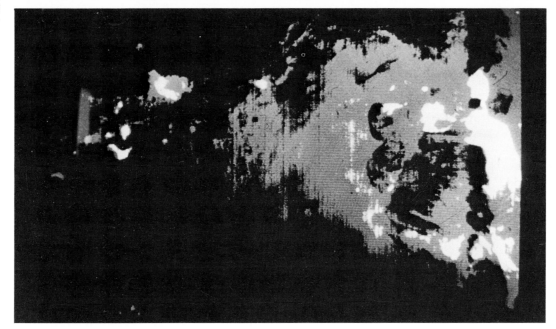

they did show that the mountain's heat profile changed very little up to the time of the massive explosion of May 18.

In contrast, similar infrared observations taken from above—from airplanes passing low over the volcano's expanding crater—did show interesting changes in heat patterns. According to Hugh Kieffer at the US Geological Survey's facility in Flagstaff, Arizona, a set of such infrared observations taken by a commercial contractor on May 16 was not processed over that weekend because of the extra cost involved. This was unfortunate because they turned out to show clear signs of heating within the summit crater and zones of increased heat flow along the margins of the summit graben. They also revealed, to the north of the crater, numerous developing hot spots, which showed that the expanding bulge in the area east of Goat Rocks had become perforated, allowing heat to escape. This suggested that extensive heating was occurring near the surface. Kieffer later told Science magazine that if the infrared images had been processed before the main eruption scientists would have "at the very least been more concerned about the possibility of a landslide" from the enlarging bulge, if only because of the potential lubricating effect of the water coming from the melting glacial ice.

The infrared images taken by Oregon National Guard aircraft on both May 17 and 18, however, showed almost no changes in the heat anomalies mapped on the 16th, even though the last infrared scanning mission was flown less than 3 hours before the cataclysmic eruption.

Once the volcano exploded, however, one of the key questions was what the aerosols emitted by the volcano might do to the earth's climate. Some scientists have suggested that enough aerosols injected into the stratosphere in the right places and at the proper altitudes might be able to reduce measurably the temperature over the entire planetary surface. Aerosols, of course, are very fine particles—either solid or liquid—that become suspended in a gas such as the atmosphere. Common types of aerosols include smoke, fog, smog, and mist. The massive loads of aerosols that originate in volcanic eruptions—and then get trapped in the circulation patterns of the stratosphere—are thought to play a role in regulating the proportions of solar energy reflected back toward space and captured by the stratosphere (directly or by absorption of radiation from the earth's surface). Such a regulatory role is of great importance because some of the smaller aerosol particles are known to remain afloat in the stratosphere for months, or even years, whereas the aerosol particles that remain aloft in the lower atmosphere, the troposphere, tend quickly to get rained out onto the ground.

As it happened, well in advance of Mount St. Helens's cataclysmic eruption, atmospheric scientists had been doing research on the chemistry, albedo, and physical nature of the stratosphere. Thus they were well prepared to analyze the eruption's impact on the atmosphere. This preparedness was not accidental, however. In recent years there has been mounting concern over the large amounts of carbon dioxide being added to the atmosphere by human activities—such as burning fossil fuels and deforestation. Some observers fear that the result will be a significant warming of the atmosphere, leading to dramatic changes in the climate and perhaps serious changes in sea levels. This, according to the most reasonable scenarios, would occur because carbon dioxide in the atmosphere tends to trap the energy in the infrared portion of the spectrum that otherwise would reradiate back into space, causing the atmosphere to heat up slowly by what is called the greenhouse effect.

There have even been warnings of a runaway greenhouse effect in which the atmospheric warming causes more water to evaporate into the atmosphere, the vapor then trapping even more heat, causing more evaporation, more trapping, and so on. Indeed, atmospheric physicists like to point to the broiling-hot atmosphere of the planet Venus as an outstanding example of a runaway greenhouse. On Venus, where temperatures are on the order of 900°F (480°C), all the volatile elements have been vaporized and are now found afloat in the tremendously dense, acid-rich atmosphere, making it almost a perfect picture of Hell.

One of the important uncertainties in this greenhouse scenario on earth, however, is the effect that the presence of aerosols—from volcanoes and other dust sources—has on the temperature of the atmosphere. It has been suggested, in fact, that human activities may be producing so much aerosol material that the warming effect caused by accumulating carbon dioxide is essen-

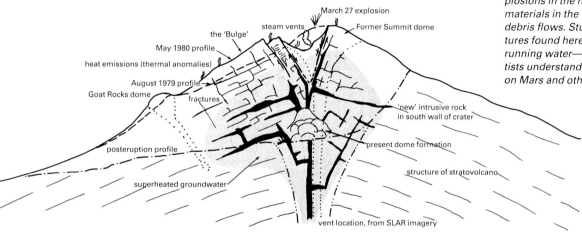

the 'Bulge'
May 1980 profile
heat emissions (thermal anomalies)
August 1979 profile
Goat Rocks dome
fractures
posteruption profile
superheated groundwater

steam vents
faults
March 27 explosion
Former Summit dome

'new' intrusive rock
in south wall of crater
present dome formation
structure of stratovolcano

vent location, from SLAR imagery

Left:
Hypothetical north–south cross section of Mount St. Helens show-ing the 1979 profile, the preerup-tion 1980 profile, and a posteruption profile.

Below:
Photograph of badlands topogra-phy created through phreatic ex-plosions in the hot pyroclastic materials in the Toutle River valley debris flows. Study of the struc-tures found here—formed without running water—may help scien-tists understand the features seen on Mars and other planets.

tially neutralized. The answer to this question, however, is still being sought through research projects such as NASA's ACE program.

This aerosol-sampling program had begun a year and a half before Mount St. Helens erupted. Its goal was to assess the climatic impact of aerosols found in the stratosphere. To this end, U-2 aircraft, in conjunction with satellite observations, were used. For example, in July, 1979, the research group had sent a sampling flight over Alaska to measure what are considered to be baseline levels for aerosols in the stratosphere.

The information collected through the Ames ACE program, both before and after the eruption, proved of tremendous value in two respects. First, it offered the most complete set of observations ever made of volcanic aerosols. And second, its U-2 data, combined with data from NASA's Stratospheric Aerosol and Gas Experiment (SAGE), made it possible to explore the atmospheric impact of volcanic eruptions such as that at Mount St. Helens.

As reported by C. B. Sear and P. M. Kelly in *Nature* shortly after the explosion of Mount St. Helens, volcanic particles can "form a veil which can cover most of a hemisphere and occasionally, after very large eruptions, the whole globe." They added that the spread of an ash veil depends on the latitude at which dust has been injected, how high it is sent into the atmosphere, the size of the dust particles themselves, and the condition of stratospheric winds at the time of eruption.

Sear and Kelly, in the Climatic Research Unit at the University of East Anglia, Norwich, England, added that as a general rule the winds in the stratosphere tend to keep dust in the Northern Hemisphere if the eruptions occur from volcanoes at mid-to-high northern latitudes, north of 30°N. When volcanoes erupt in tropical latitudes, however, stratospheric circulation tends to spread the veil of dust over the whole globe, as happened after the eruptions of Krakatau in 1883 and Agung (Bali) in 1963.

They noted, too, that the dust from Mount St. Helens could spread over more of the globe than might normally have been expected, since the month of May, when Mount St. Helens exploded, exhibits the largest flow of lower stratospheric air toward the equator.

In addition to sampling these important aerosol loads, however, the U-2 was also used as a camera platform for photographic missions above the volcano. For a whole month after the May 18 eruption, in fact, personnel at the Ames Research Center kept an eye on weather maps, looking for clear skies that would allow pictures of the damage to be taken from an altitude of 65,000 feet (19.8 kilometers). This photographic exercise was carried out at the request of the Washington State Office of Emergency Services and was accomplished under the Ames Western Regional Applications Program.

Pictures from this effort gave State of Washington officials their first comprehensive coverage of the damaged area. This was possible to achieve rather quickly because from 65,000 feet altitude the U-2's cameras can resolve features as small as 5 feet (1.5 meters) in diameter, and each of the 9-inch by 18-inch (228-millimeter by 457-millimeter) frames of film covers a ground area measuring 4 miles by 8 miles (6.4 kilometers by 13 kilometers).

When the sampling of the stratosphere began, almost immediately after the eruption of May 18, the data indicated that the air over central California had not yet been affected by the flow of ash and gases into the stratosphere. But by May 29, once the aerosol particles from the mountain had circled the earth, aerosols were observed over California at 43,000 feet (13 kilometers) altitude. This material—rich in ash particles and sulfuric acid—was similar to what had been measured in the ash plume as it came from the volcano. At altitudes above 43,000 feet, however, the stratosphere remained essentially clear of the volcano's aerosol particles.

Preliminary data from the first five stratospheric sampling missions into the Mount St. Helens plume indicated that the volcanic plume contained a variable mixture of solid ash particles and sulfuric acid, with the proportions changing with time and location. Indeed, the amount of sulfuric acid found afloat in the stratosphere turned out to be several hundred times greater than had been measured before the eruption.

A research group from the National Center for Atmospheric Research (NCAR), Boulder, Colorado—B. W. Gandrud and A. L. Lazrus—remarked after analyzing results from the U-2 experiment flown on May 19 that their "exposed filter papers, which

The first puff of light gray ash enters the base of the dark eruption plume at 11:47 A.M. during the huge eruption of May 18, 1980.

normally appear white, were quite discolored, ranging from a brownish gray at 17.7 kilometers (altitude) to a reddish brown at 13.1 kilometers. In other stratospheric sampling we have never observed a discoloration of the filters."

In analysis of their data after a flight on May 22, the NCAR researchers said that "the results . . . indicate very large enhancements, up to 216 times background sulfate. The particulate chloride is enhanced at 20.1 kilometers [altitude]."

In their report in *Science* magazine, the Colorado-based team stated that "the flight on 17 June, which was designed to sample debris from the first eruption (May 18) after it had passed around the world once, showed that the particulate sulfate levels were still enhanced, although not nearly as much as on the 22 May flight."

It was also noted that

most of the ash particles—which are likely to be made more massive by coatings of ice—were found to leave the stratospheric plume from Mt. St. Helens within several days, probably also causing a selective depletion of chloride relative to sulfur. Though the particulate chloride seems to be consistently enhanced during the earliest stages, the resulting enhancement of stratospheric chloride concentrations after extensive mixing of the plume throughout the stratosphere should be very small. This also applies to the acid chloride vapor concentrations in the plume.

We do not know the extent to which the eruption plume was initially enriched in hydrochloric acid, but observations continue to suggest that major eruptions do not significantly enhance stratospheric acid chloride levels.

While more study is obviously necessary, that finding may prove important in the continuing, rather bitter debate over the role of chlorine—both natural and anthropogenic—in controlling the persistent layer of ozone that resides at midstratospheric altitudes. Concern over depletion of the ozone layer—with a resultant increase in the flux of ultraviolet radiation reaching the ground—has already led to restrictions on the use of chlorofluorocarbons, meaning Freon, as the propellant in spray cans. The argument over the justification of such restrictions has involved strong disagreement on the quantity of chlorine injected into the atmosphere naturally through volcanic action.

A team from the Ames Research Center—Neil H. Farlow, Verne R. Oberbeck, Kenneth G. Snetsinger, and Guy V. Ferry—along with George Polkowski and Dennis M. Hayes from the LFE Corporation in Richmond, California, gathered data on the size distributions and mineralogy of ash particles in the stratosphere, using the U-2 aircraft. As reported in their article in *Science* magazine, they found that

ash particles obtained one day after the eruption of 18 May, 1980, were completely dry, whereas all ash collected later was covered with acid. . . . The dry ash samples obtained over Montana at 14 and 17 kilometers [altitude] are composed of angular grains ranging in size from around one-tenth of a micron to as large as 30 microns, with median size around three-tenths micron. . . .

Although the first samples of ash were very dry, flow marks in dust on the aircraft wings suggested that there were zones within the cloud containing large amounts of liquid, presumably acid, associated with the ash. The second flight to Montana, on 22 May, four days after the initial [big] eruption, provided an ash sample flooded with acid. Collecting wires were completely coated on the flight-facing side with coalesced acid drops encasing ash grains.

Another surprising finding, announced by C. F. Rogers, J. G. Hudson, and W. C. Kocmond, from the Desert Research Institute in Reno, Nevada, was that "cloud condensation nuclei" were much more abundant, by an order of magnitude, than expected. This, they wrote in a report that also appeared in *Science* magazine, suggests "that volcanoes may be an important source of cloud condensation nuclei in the lower stratosphere, both by direct injection of cloud condensation nuclei" and by supplying the materials that can combine to form cloud condensation nuclei. These nuclei are described as particles that act as points around which water vapor can condense to form droplets. The presence of such nuclei at high altitude, they said, could modify the microstructure of clouds, changing normal rain processes and perhaps altering the scattering and absorption of sunlight.

Ash particles, some as large as 30 microns in diameter, were found to be chemically similar to the ash found on the ground near the volcano. As time went on, however, the larger particles apparently were falling out of the air, and on later missions the largest aerosol particles found in the stratosphere were only 3 microns in diameter.

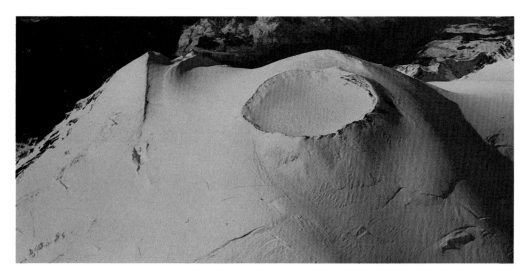

Above:
Summit crater atop Mount Rainier, in Washington State.

Right:
Mount Jefferson, as seen from the north.

Far right:
In northern California, the Black Butte cinder cone, in foreground, flanks tall Mount Shasta and the Shastina cone.

Far left:
The tenacious ash particles cling to the needles of a fir tree 6 months after the main eruption of Mount St. Helens. Needles covered by ash turned brown and died, but new shoots that emerged bright green after ashfalls had subsided testify that the tree still lives.

Left:
Observers near the mountain can see that the ashfall consists of two distinct layers. The bottom layer is made up of a fine-grained dark material, old ash, that was removed explosively from the Mount St. Helens crater. The higher layer consists of newer, lighter-colored ash and pumice blocks. The surface has been covered by a slightly darker material—again, ash and pumice—that came from later eruptions during dome-building activity.

Above:
View of the devastated forest lands some 6 miles (9 kilometers) northeast of the crater.

Right:
Rapidly colonizing natural vegetation sprouts vigorously from parallel erosion gullies on a hillside northwest of Mount St. Helens.

Geomorphologists working for the US Forest Service survey an area on Clearwater Ridge, planning to set up an experiment for the study of erosion rates within the devastated area near the volcano.

Right:
Photograph of the July 22 eruption, as viewed from the northwest at about 9:30 P.M.

Below:
Group of hummocks, sometimes more than 115 feet (35 meters) high, dwarfed the researchers who ventured in to examine the surface of the debris flows.

Above right:
Photograph of the Dome-zilla structure at its maximum height of about 450 feet (135 meters) on February 7, 1981.

Below right:
View of Mount St. Helens from the northeast on February 7, 1981.

High-altitude research plane, a U-2 operated by the National Aeronautics and Space Administration, is shown high above San Francisco Bay, California. (Photo by NASA)

Above:
Spirit Lake as seen from the top of the expanding bulge on April 30, 1981.

Below:
Spirit Lake as seen from a helicopter while hovering over the gap in the north wall of the Mount St. Helens crater, May 28, 1980.

Scientists involved in the ACE program also reported that large increases in gaseous sulfur dioxide were measured. This gas, which issues directly from the volcanic vent, is thought to serve as a source for the sulfuric acid that was detected. The chemistry is thought to be driven by sunlight.

During the U-2's first flight over the volcano, shortly after the huge explosive eruption of May 18, sulfur dioxide levels were found to be between ten and 1,000 times above normal background levels. On the second flight, the sulfur dioxide levels were at about 100 times background, and it was discovered that water vapor levels within the plume were at least 10 times higher than normal. This latter measurement suggested that a large amount of water—either ground water from inside the shattered peak, or from water trapped in the magma itself—was being injected into the stratosphere.

Even before the main eruption of May 18, Dartmouth College volcanologists Richard Stoiber, Stanley Williams, and Lawrence Malinconico were flying above the crater trying to measure the amount of sulfur dioxide being released. They found that the mountain was releasing perhaps 30 tons of sulfur dioxide per day during the early steam eruptions. This rate of release was quite low compared to the hundreds of thousands of tons per day of sulfur dioxide released during eruption of other volcanoes. Since this low level of gas emissions had not been seen before during an eruption, Stoiber and his colleagues concluded that the action was coming only from groundwater within the peak, which was being heated to cause steam explosions. This idea tended to agree with conclusions reached by US Geological Survey scientists through other methods.

Malinconico told a *Science* magazine reporter that he had expected to see increased releases of gases before an eruption involving new magma occurred, something he had observed during three eruptions of Mount Etna. After the huge explosion of May 18, however, he said the lack of a large flow of gases was not surprising because the mountain had been able to contain the magma and all the trapped gases until the instant of explosion.

Actually, perhaps the most ominous sign that something big was coming came from the bulge on the volcano's north flank. The change in the shape of the Goat Rocks area was not noticed at first, but after the minor steam eruption of March 27 the uplifting became obvious even to the naked eye. By mid-April photogrametric observations were showing the north side of the mountain was expanding outward and upward at a steady rate of about 5 feet (1.5 meters) per day.

The bulge's dramatic rate of expansion was finally measured by James Moore and Donald Swanson of the US Geological Survey in Menlo Park, and Peter Lipman of the agency's Denver office. They made their measurements by comparing a series of separate contour maps that had been prepared as the bulge increased in size. These maps had been drawn on the basis of repeated photographs of 14 targets that had been placed on the bulge.

"It was just incredible," commented Albert Eggers, of Puget Sound University. "You could see the mountain go up, and here we were working just a half-mile away." Moore explained that the expansion of the bulge, while rapid and dramatic, was absolutely uniform, apparently filling with a few million cubic meters of magma daily for several weeks. Up to the time of the large blast, too, the rate of expansion remained unchanged.

In fact, Moore and his colleagues were expecting some sort of change in the expansion rate, which would signal that the rock and ice of the bulge were about to slide off the mountain. This is the way it was expected to act. The mountain never got a chance to exhibit that change, however, because an earthquake of about Richter magnitude 5 intervened, triggering collapse of the bulge, sending it sliding down into the Toutle River valley.

This eruption, a directed blast, has often been compared to the explosion of a huge atomic bomb, but Robert Decker, director of the Geological Survey's Hawaiian Volcano Observatory, commented that it was actually more like the explosion of a huge steam boiler. As he explained it, the removal of overlying rock sharply reduced pressure on the superheated ground water inside the mountain, allowing it to flash into steam. The clouds of steam sped down the mountain's slopes at tremendous speeds, laden with rock debris and ash, devastating everything in their path. As the steam burst loose, it rapidly tore rock away from the mountain, relieving pressure on the magma, causing explosive release of the magmatic gases.

Robert Wesson, assistant director of the US Geological Survey, commented to *Science* reporter Richard Kerr that "in retrospect, we perhaps underestimated what the bulge was trying to tell us. If we were to see it again, we'd take the bulge a lot more seriously."

Even though they did not know what it meant at the time, the hazard alert issued on April 30 by the US Geological Survey did point out that the bulge was "the most serious potential hazard posed by the current volcanic activity at Mount St. Helens." What the USGS scientists meant, however, was that the bulge might let loose an enormous avalanche of ice and rock that could injure spectators who ventured too close. They had no way of knowing that the whole side of the mountain would suddenly slip away, essentially uncorking the violently effervescent gases locked in magma within the mountain.

It was the dissolved gas content, of course, that pulverized the magma, producing the fine ash particles that went soaring to such heights. Volcano researchers have long known that the magma associated with Mount St. Helens's eruptions—dacite—is particularly explosive because of its high viscosity and its high gas content. According to Andrei Sarna-Wojcicki, at the Geological Survey's Menlo Park, California, facility, samples from Mount St. Helens showed the ash to be composed of 67 to 70 percent silica, 17 to 18 percent alumina, 4 percent calcium oxide, 3 to 4 percent iron oxide, 2 percent potassium oxide, and some other minor trace elements. Such magmas, when so rich in silica, Sarna-Wojcicki explained, tend to become highly polymerized and therefore viscous—several orders of magnitude more viscous than water. When silica content exceeds 65 percent, the viscosity becomes so great that dissolved gases cannot escape. When such conditions develop—as they did beneath Mount St. Helens—it becomes possible for increasing gas pressure eventually to blow the top off the mountain. At Mount St. Helens, of course, pressure was released by the north face of the mountain sliding away.

The pulverized ash from Mount St. Helens's eruption immediately caused concern for health reasons. Since the ash contained so much silica, since it was being repeatedly stirred up into the air by wind and automobile traffic, and since so much of it was present as respirable-size particles, health authorities immediately began looking into its potential as a causative factor in a chronically disabling disease called silicosis. Analysis soon indicated that fully half of the ash particles were in the respirable-size range (less than 10 microns). And, according to Richard Landingham at the Lawrence Livermore Laboratory in California, that was reason for concern.

As it turned out, however, only about 2 percent of the silica appeared to be in the quartz phase, which is most dangerous, and most of the silica was bound up in the less threatening form of sodium aluminum silicate feldspar. In addition, hospital officials in the areas of heaviest ashfall reported no serious increases in respiratory problems, at least in the beginning.

In looking back over the historical records, volcanologists suspect that the eruption most closely resembling what happened at Mount St. Helens occured in 1956 at the Bezymianny volcano in Soviet Kamchatka. In that event, they said, seismic activity closely paralleled what was recorded in the Pacific Northwest, with earthquake activity accelerating, then reaching a peak and tapering off to an almost constant level. Also, at both Mount St. Helens and Bezymianny, toward the end of the active seismic period there was no obvious, immediate warning before part of the mountain was blasted away. And in both cases, after that several smaller, but still violent, eruptions followed as lava domes were being built inside the existing craters.

But given time, support, and much work, scientists may be expected to surpass the knowledge of volcanoes gleaned from such historical records by studying the eruption of Mount St. Helens. It has been said, probably correctly, that the activity at Mount St. Helens quickly became the best-studied eruption in history. Nonetheless, even a year after the huge blast of May 18, 1980, it was still too early to begin listing the discoveries—and the bits of new understanding—that emerged as a result of this work. It is certain, of course, that in the history of the science of volcanology Mount St. Helens will stand out as a real landmark, an opportunity for research that was quickly, expertly seized upon by a well-trained, well-equipped army of eager specialists.

As should be expected, too, and as demonstrated by the US space program, many of the benefits of this reserach effort will show up much later in more distantly related research fields. The devastated area around the volcano, for example, turned out to be an almost perfect natural laboratory for the study of a variety of phenomena, including the development and evolution of terrestrial and aquatic ecosystems, erosional processes, and the dynamics of microclimates.

Another positive outcome of the eruption of Mount St. Helens that should be noted is that it brought together a band of prestigious volcanologists, geophysicists, geomorphologists, petrochemists, atmospheric physicists, biologists, hydrologists, sociologists, geographers, and other specialists. Although, as suggested by geologist Robert Yeats of Oregon State University, the depth of information could have been improved by even broader contact within the scientific community as a whole, the US Geological Survey must be commended for its competent, highly professional performance. Not only did the USGS function as an adviser to agencies involved in protecting public safety, but the Geological Survey also collected a massive amount of information that should, in time, benefit the effort to predict volcanic eruptions and understand the volcanic activities of the Cascade system.

Mount St. Helens has shown us the *gestalt* effect of interdisciplinary research work. The aftermath of this gigantic explosion has seen the growth of a broad dialogue among the various specialists and a unification of divergent disciplines around a common event. Educators also report there has been a sudden, encouraging resurgence of the public's curiosity about scientific subjects, probably as a result of the daily volcanology "lessons" provided by the mountain and the news media.

In addition, the events surrounding the eruption led directly to rapid expansion of the active, well-managed Washington Seismic Networks run by the University of Washington in Seattle. The seismic networks' on-line, computerized seismic recording system—capable of digitizing 100 samples per second—has yielded useful summaries of the magnitudes and frequencies of seismic events for the whole region. Also, automatic mapping of earthquake hypocenters has yielded important new clues about volcanism in the Cascades.

An illustrative example are the remarks made by Prof. Steve Malone of the University of Washington during a symposium on Mount St. Helens. Malone noted that each of the major eruptions of the volcano had been accompanied by uniquely different patterns of seismicity, but that in every case each eruption had been preceded by some obvious seismic precursor event. Before the large landslide that apparently triggered the May 18 lateral blast, for instance, it was abundantly clear that a magnitude 5.1 earthquake about 0.8 miles (1.3 kilometers) below a hot, unstable "bulge" could turn loose the mass of rock and ice perched so unstably on the mountain. So the landslide trigger hypothesis, advanced by USGS scientists days before it actually happened, had been entirely logical and clearly justified.

Actually, that initial slide probably contained about 400,000 cubic yards (half a cubic kilometer) of rock and ice, so that it acted rather like a pressure-control valve that was suddenly opened. The removal of the heavy cover caused sudden decompression of the superheated, water-saturated rock within the mountain. Thus the newly exposed rock was literally blown apart by the water as it flashed into steam, unburdening even more superheated rock below. Over a period of perhaps 10 minutes, the series of explosions worked their way down into the core of the mountain.

Also, 2 minutes after the initial triggering earthquake a second temblor was recorded. This was probably caused by the large, devastating lateral blast that pushed much of the mountain's hot core down into the Toutle River valley. This was the massively destructive debris flow.

Unfortunately, neither the earlier seismic events nor heat measurements taken of the mountain gave direct early warning when the event was coming, or how big it might be. Nonetheless, both the seismicity and the heat patterns did indicate rather clearly the location of the probable activity even a month before the explosion.

In addition, other phenomena associated with the eruption will also become increasingly important as we increase our understanding of what occurred at Mount St. Helens. While flying near the eruptive plume, shortly after noon on the day of the major eruption, observers noticed an abrupt color change in th column of ash, steam, and gas rising from the crater. It was found later that this change apparently correlated with a sudden increase in seismic harmonic tremor. This event may thus have marked a change from phreatic expansion of the crater as it became a major magmatic eruption. Also that afternoon, our SLAR (side-looking airborne radar) images clearly located the vent in operation, but after 6 P.M. we failed to see any major eruptive center. This change appears to correlate well with a marked tapering off of the harmonic tremor, which occurred about 5:30 P.M.

Subsequent eruptions have shown two distinctly different types of seismic precursors. When the seismic signals were harmonic tremors, the volcano's vent seemed to be open during the eruption, and the activity included pyroclastic flows and large discharges of ash into the air, as on May 25, June 12, and August 7. But when the vent had been plugged by a lava dome—and also prior to the big May 18 eruption—shallow earthquakes were the main precursory events, as on July 22 and October 16.

An important point made by Malone at the Mount St. Helens symposium was that while the computers and the complementary data from numerous sources do help with short-term prediction, the really critical element in the monitoring effort has been experienced personnel. It was the human factor that was often most important in interpreting complex and often confusing data.

It must be noted, however, that with the benefit of hindsight, in many ways the prediction of an eruption at Mount St. Helens was a cinch. After all, two months of rather vigorous, unusual seismic activity, and the obvious inflation of the mountain's northeast flank by more than 300 feet (90 meters), were warning enough that something big was going on. In addition, the entire eruption scenario was pretty well known just from study of the past 4,500-year history of the mountain. We were well aware that Mount St. Helens was still alive, still active, and in danger of erupting at any time. The mountain gave ample warning, and it was well known how dangerous it could be.

As for the danger to the public of such eruptions, there has been some criticism of state and federal authorities for not making the closed red zone around the mountain larger and for not being more emphatic in warning sightseers away. But it is probably safe to say that many people were not willing to accept such warnings. Few seemed willing to believe that an eruption might reach the magnitude it did, even though evidence from the volcano's history made that possibility quite clear.

We should also be aware, of course, that the effects of such predictions—if heeded by the public—can have serious impact on industry, including the tourist industry. Predictions, then, should be made and released with some care. But we should not let such considerations stand in the way of public safety. If scientists believe events of such magnitude are imminent and dangerous, then the predictions should be made and the warnings should be heeded, whatever the costs.

Given all we have learned, we should be confident that when future volcanic eruptions occur we shall be able to recognize the danger in time to provide timely, useful warning. This should be kept in mind as modern societies become ever more complex, ever more interdependent, and thus ever more vulnerable to dramatic environmental events like the eruption of Mount St. Helens.

A Mohawk aerial surveillance aircraft approaches Mount St. Helens on one of the continuing remote-sensing missions that help to monitor changes in the volcano's activity. (Photo by Grumman Aircraft Co.)

Technical Vignette: Perturbations of the atmosphere by the blast
Albert E. Frank

Air, like water, is a fluid. A stone dropped in water produces a series of waves that ripple outward from the disturbance. In an analogous fashion, the May 18th explosion of Mount St. Helens generated waves that propagated through the atmosphere away from the mountain. The waves (called gravity waves) revealed their presence by producing pressure oscillations on barometers throughout the Pacific Northwest. The extreme magnitude of the pressure change is attributable to Toledo being only about 65 kilometers northwest of Mount St. Helens (facing the side of the mountain that blew out). Sensitive barographs at Washington, DC, and De Bilt, Netherlands, recorded the arrival of the waves 3 hours, 20 minutes, and 7 hours, 7 minutes, respectively, after the eruption. The amplitude of the pressure change at Washington was 0.06 inches of mercury; at De Bilt the pressure oscillation had an amplitude of 0.01 inches.

To put these values in some perspective, note that a pressure change of 0.20 inches would be experienced by ascending 180 feet above the ground (near sea level); a severe thunderstorm will cause a pressure change of about 0.10 inches; sounds sufficiently strong to cause pain have pressure waves with amplitudes around 0.02 inches. In comparing Mount St. Helens with the cataclysmic eruption of Krakatoa in 1883, it is interesting to note that the captain of a ship 50 miles from Krakatoa observed that "the mercurial barometer did not stand still for a single moment, but incessantly went up and down from 28 to 30 inches."

Study of the pressure changes indicates that the initial eruption of Mount St. Helens was equivalent to the explosion of several megatons of TNT. It might seem likely that persons near Mount St. Helens on Sunday morning, May 18, would have heard a deafening roar as the eruption commenced. In actuality however, those closest to the volcano heard little or no noise from the blast, while the eruption was clearly heard hundreds of miles from the mountain. (The eruption of Krakatoa was clearly heard 4,800 kilometers from the volcano!) This apparent paradox occurred because (1) the speed of sound is faster in warm air than in cold air; and (2) at about 10 kilometers above sea level the air temperature stops decreasing with height, becoming warmer with increasing altitude. Upon reaching this warm air (the stratosphere), the sound waves from the eruption were refracted toward the ground. The eruption was described as sounding like sonic booms, thunder, and heavy artillery.

The GOES-West (geostationary operational environmental) satellite is in geosynchronous orbit 35,800 kilometers above the earth. Every half-hour it photographs the visible disk of the earth to provide cloud photographs for use in weather forecasting. Only 6 minutes after the eruption began, the ash cloud already extended 100 kilometers from the mountain. The satellite images showed growth of the ash cloud in the following 90 minutes, and a white ring surrounding the ash plume was probably created by clouds formed by pressure waves generated by the blast. The ring expanded away from the volcano and was difficult

to detect 2 hours later. Later images taken at 2-hour intervals showed the cloud of ash as it followed the winds aloft, first heading east, then turning southward into western Montana and eastern Idaho. (An upper level ridge of high pressure in eastern Oregon caused the winds and the ash cloud to move in a clockwise-curving arc.)

More than 30 hours after the eruption, the ash cloud reached the Texas Panhandle, and the ash cloud was seen stretching from western Oklahoma into southwestern South Dakota. Ash was also located over much of Wyoming, northern and western Montana, and central Idaho.

The ash passing over the central United States was at an altitude of about 12 kilometers. A lower ash plume headed toward the Gulf Coast and then turned to the northeast and traveled out over the Atlantic Ocean. The ash cloud circled the world in about 15 days. The higher clouds of debris followed a different trajectory, moving northwestward into western Canada and the Gulf of Alaska.

An especially dramatic picture was taken 82 minutes after the eruption by the NOAA-6 weather satellite in polar orbit 1,470 kilometers above the earth. The rapid growth of the cloud and its turbulent appearance indicated the violence of the event occurring below. The top of the cloud was about 19 kilometers above sea level.

Because the material discharged from Mount St. Helens was hotter than the air surrounding it, the eruption cloud experienced an upward buoyancy force. This buoyancy, plus the force of the eruption itself, propelled volcanic debris to as high as 22 kilometers above sea level, or 19 kilometers above the top of the mountain, at speeds that may have been as great as 105 meters per second. The cauliflower-like appearance of the eruption column is commonly seen in convective atmospheric circulations. When the upward momentum of the gas and ash was finally checked, the material formed the broad flat cloud that was visible in satellite pictures.

The jet of material rushing aloft created a circulation system that pulled the surrounding air into it. Air flowing up the slopes of the mountain at times created a cloud of ash around the rim of the decapitated volcano.

The effects of the ash plume on the weather at locations beneath it are well documented in the weather records from Yakima, Washington. Day was turned into night as the ash cloud screened out the sun, checking the normal morning rise of temperature and lowering visibility to near zero. Throughout the night temperatures remained constant because the ash prevented the normal escape to space of infrared radiation emitted by the earth's surface. A tipping bucket rain gauge recording showed the accumulated weight of the ash falling on Yakima was equivalent (by weight) to 0.41 inches of rain.

Pendulous clouds, similar to the mammatus clouds often seen on the underside of thunderstorm anvils, hung down from the ash plume. Frequent lightning occurred from the cloud of ash, probably as a result of friction between ash particles. An observer of the initial eruption described hundreds of lightning bolts reaching the ground from the cloud.

The late spring of 1980 was cool and wet in Oregon and Washington, and many people blamed the inclement weather on Mount St. Helens. This idea was probably strengthened by the fact that May 18 was sunny and warm, and then clouds and rain spread over the region during the next two days. Also, the eruption on June 12 spread ash over Portland, Oregon, on a night when that city also received nearly an inch of rain. What effects, if any, did the eruptions of Mount St. Helens have on precipitation and climate in the Pacific Northwest and elsewhere?

Much of the precipitation that falls in middle latitudes originally forms as snow. Snow begins to form when appropriate types of particulate matter in the atmosphere cause drops of supercooled water to freeze. Cloud droplets also form around small particles found in the air. However, a particle that is an efficient cloud-droplet nucleus usually is not a good agent for initiating snowflake growth. To date, research indicates that ash from Mount St. Helens was not very effective in stimulating formation of snow at the temperatures occurring in the clouds over the Pacific Northwest in the spring and summer of 1980.

The ash particles, though, were found to be suitable nuclei for the growth of cloud droplets. Even though the ash appears to have caused an increase in the amount of cloud drops, it probably did nqt increase precipitation. In order for raindrops to grow from cloud droplets, the cloud must contain droplets in a range of different sizes. Cloud drops that formed around ash particles tended to be mostly of the same size. It is even possible that this lack of droplet-size variety may have decreased the amount of rain that would otherwise have fallen.

Ash, gas, and water vapor deposited in the stratosphere by volcanic eruptions will remain there for months or years. This material could increase the amount of sunlight reflected back into space and might thereby cause lower temperatures over large parts of the world. The huge eruption of Mount Agung did produce a decrease in the brightness of the sun as seen from the earth's surface. However, much of this decrease was compensated for by increased amounts of sunlight scattered to earth by the ash (that is, increased sky brightness). The net effect was a slight decrease in solar radiation, but no more of a decrease than observed in years when there were no significant eruptions. The mean global temperature decreased by about 0.3°C following the eruption of Mount Agung.

Most large volcanic eruptions are followed within six to twelve months by a cooling of about 0.5°C. But since this temperature change is similar in magnitude to those that occur in years without eruptions, it is difficult to tell how much of the cooling would have occurred even if there was no volcanic activity.

It has been estimated that Krakatoa erupted 18 cubic kilometers of ash into the atmosphere and that 4 cubic kilometers of debris were ejected from Mount Agung. The volume of material from the May 18 eruption of Mount St. Helens is believed to be only 1 cubic kilometer. This suggests that any effect that Mount St. Helens might have on climate will probably be so small as to go undetected.

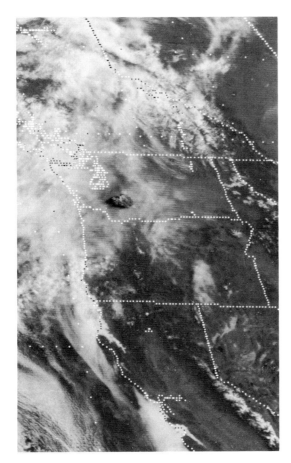

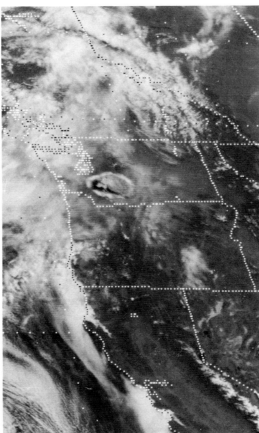

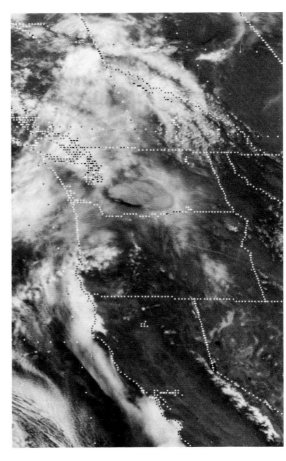

8:45 A.M. PDT
Eruption + 0 hr. 6 min.

9:15 A.M. PDT
Eruption + 0 hr. 36 min.

10:15 A.M. PDT
Eruption + 1 hr. 36 min.

GOES-West satellite image shows
the development of the ash plume
following the eruption of Mount St.
Helens (see text).

 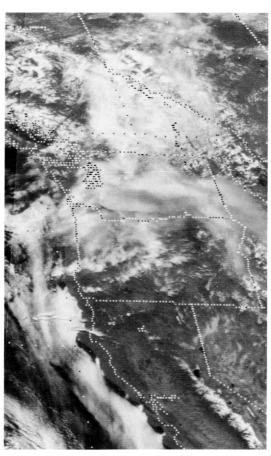 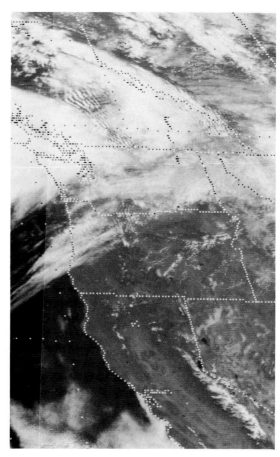

12:15 P.M. PDT
Eruption + 3 hr. 36 min.

2:15 P.M. PDT
Eruption + 5 hr. 36 min.

3:15 P.M. PDT
Eruption + 30 hr. 36 min.

NOAA-6 image taken 82 minutes after the explosive eruption of Mount St. Helens shows the violent upward expansion of the plume to a height of 12 miles (19 kilometers) above the volcano.

Technical Vignette: Prediction
Robert S. Yeats

Geologists are the historians of the earth, bent on exploring its past and using the knowledge of the past to search for hidden resources. Only recently have geologists been asked by society to use the past to predict the future. It is true that we know a great deal about the earth, but unfortunately we do not know enough to make predictions with any certainty.

We got into the prediction business with earthquakes, and that was less than 10 years ago. Despite a major effort, earth scientists in the United States have yet to make a major earthquake prediction that saved lives and property. A prediction was made in 1976 that a major earthquake might strike the Los Angeles area in the following year. That prediction was a false alarm.

Only the Chinese have predicted earthquakes successfully, and their predictions have saved thousands of lives. But the Chinese failed to predict their worst earthquake of the decade, the Tangshan earthquake of 1976, which resulted in the deaths of hundreds of thousands of people. They blamed this prediction failure on The Gang of Four!

We know much less about volcanoes than we do about earthquakes. One of the main reasons for this is that most people have failed to take volcanoes seriously: a death here and an injury there, sustained mainly by people who got too close; people get killed by a volcano because they try to farm on its slopes, and this happens primarily in Third World countries like Indonesia and the Philippines. And

Reprinted by permission from the *Oregonian*, December 7, 1980.

in the United States, most dangerous volcanoes are in Alaska, far from populated areas, while the Cascade volcanoes had been quiet for more than a century. Mount St. Helens, of course, changed all that.

Over the years a few (US) scientists persisted in the study of volcanic hazards, even though not many people in the United States took them seriously. One result of the persistence of Rocky Crandell and Don Mullineaux of the US Geological Survey was a long-range prediction that Mount St. Helens might become active before the end of the century. That prediction was based mainly on the past history of Mount St. Helens. It had built its cone in the past 1,000 to 2,000 years and it had erupted every hundred years or so for much of that period. Crandell and Mullineaux saw no reason why this past history of frequent eruptions would not persist into the future.

The importance of this prediction is that it set apart Mount St. Helens as a more dangerous volcano than others in the Cascades. When activity finally began last March (1980), scientists were already conditioned to believe that an eruption could happen there. As a result, a volcano watch team was assembled quickly by the USGS. Thanks to Crandell and Mullineaux's report, the scientific community in the Pacific Northwest recognized as early as late March 1980 that a major eruption was possible, and the public was so informed.

The seismic activity and the ash and steam eruptions of late March and early April led to a second, intermediate-range prediction. This prediction stated that the volcano was in a dangerous condition and might undergo a major eruption in the next few weeks or months. As a result, a Red Zone was established, limiting access to Mount St. Helens and to the major roads leading to the volcano.

The *Oregonian*, in its article "A Terrible Beauty," questioned the effectiveness of that prediction and of the access restrictions, and also observed that the restricted area was far too small. However, it seems to me that without the intermediate-range prediction, Spirit Lake and the Upper Toutle River valley would have been crowded with people on that beautiful spring Sunday morning in May, and hundreds of people, rather than dozens, would have been killed. There were no troops of Boy Scouts or organized YMCA camp groups, no church retreats, no crowded campgrounds at Spirit Lake or on the upper Toutle.

On that May weekend, hundreds of climbers, myself among them, ascended Mount Hood. Without the warning and the public response to it, other hundreds of climbers might have been ascending Mount St. Helens on that day, negotiating the new crevasses caused by earthquakes and the great bulge.

So the long-range and intermediate-range predictions paid for all the federal support ever given for research into volcanic hazards many times over.

What about the short-range prediction?

A short-range prediction states that a volcano will erupt in a matter of hours and everyone should be evacuated. That prediction was not made. Looking back over the data available on May 18, we still cannot identify a smoking gun that should have caused the alarm to be raised.

The seismology group at the University of Washington went through a period of bleak depression in late May and early June as they sifted back through their records to find the clue that eluded them in mid-May, the clue that would have blown the whistle and got everybody out that Sunday morning. They still have not found it. The number of large earthquakes around Mount St. Helens had been decreasing slowly ever since March 26, before the first puff of ash. There had been an increase in the magnitude of some of the earthquakes. But was that enough evidence to sound the alarm?

In late April the volcano stopped erupting ash for over two weeks, and helicopters bearing Portland television cameramen and Portland State University geologists made landings on the rim of the crater. Governor Dixy Lee Ray (of Washington State) was under increasing pressure to allow homeowners access to their property in the upper Toutle valley. Some people wondered whether the eruption might be over.

Infrared photographs that registered heat coming out of the volcano were being taken in April and May. The *Oregonian* article attached great significance to the fact that infrared photographs taken by Hugh Kieffer of the USGS on Friday, May 16, were not developed until the day after the eruption. The article implied that prompt development of these photographs might have led to a warning, at least of a massive landslide.

The Oregon National Guard, using Mohawk OV-1 reconnaissance aircraft, had also been taking infrared photos of Mount St. Helens. The Guard flew photo missions during the predawn hours of May 17 and 18, and the photographs were developed as soon as the aircraft returned to Salem (Oregon) and completed the missions on the morning of May 18. Chuck Rosenfeld, a geomorphologist at Oregon State University and photo interpretation officer for the Oregon National Guard, noted the increased amount of heat on the May 18 photo as compared to May 17. This information was transmitted to the USGS by telephone about the same time that the eruptive blast occurred. After looking at both sets of infrared photographs, I doubt that a short-range prediction would have been made on that basis alone. The photographs suggested a build-up of heat, it is true, but a prediction based on them would have been for landslides or mudslides or possibly a new ash eruption.

A short-range prediction is the toughest to make because it has the greatest social impact. It requires that a danger area be marked out and that everyone—residents, visitors, loggers—leave the area. Crandell and Mullineaux had predicted that the major river valleys west of Mount St. Helens, including the Toutle and Lewis rivers, might be subject to major mudflows. A short-range prediction would have meant evacuation of these valleys, probably as far west as Interstate Highway 5. A prediction would have meant convincing governmental authorities that evacuation was necessary at a time when these authorities were under increasing pressure to open up the Toutle River valley to the public.

The team of scientists assembled by the Geological Survey at Vancouver and Seattle, Washington, was responsible for making this prediction. As indicated to me later in the summer by Chief Scientist Don Peterson, the USGS staff and the money to maintain this staff were drawn on an emergency basis from other projects. There was much to be done and very few people to do it.

There is no doubt in my mind that the USGS sent in its best people to work on Mount St. Helens. The roster at Vancouver included Jim Moore, Bill Melson, Pete Lipman, Bob Christiansen, Bob Decker, Don Mullineaux, Rocky Crandell, Don Peterson, Dave Johnston—a Who's Who of research volcanologists.

But there was not enough time to sit back and evaluate the information coming in from Mount St. Helens—complex information about the great bulge above Goat Rocks, changes in the chemical composition of the gases being emitted by steam fumaroles near the summit, changes in the earth's gravity on the north slope, changes in the location and character of the thousands of earthquakes being received by the geophysics group at the University of Washington. There was no chance to compare what was happening at Mount St. Helens with other volcanoes around the world.

The Geological Survey was criticized for keeping Mount St. Helens to itself and for failing to bring other volcano experts in the Northwest into the emergency team assembled at Vancouver in March and April. I am not concerned here about USGS and US Forest Service restrictions affecting scientific research by geologists outside the USGS. I am concerned about whether the restrictive policy affected the ability of the scientific community at large to predict the May 18 eruption.

I know of no qualified scientist who has come forward with the claim that he (or she) predicted the May 18 blast and that the prediction was ignored by the USGS. Geologists known to me were predicting some kind of eruption based mainly upon the continued growth of the bulge, but most people predicted a large landslide, perhaps accompanied by a major ash eruption and the appearance of a lava dome.

Most geologists also predicted that new magmatic products would appear sooner or later, either as volcanic ash, a lava dome, or pyroclastic flows. A blast was considered as no more than an outside possibility. In this regard, the predictions of non-USGS geologists living in the region were no different from those of the USGS.

The fact is we saw nothing in the data that would have led to a prediction that a major eruption was due in a few hours or days. The best we might have done was take more seriously the prospects of a

major lateral blast out of the north side toward Spirit Lake. We might have made a major effort to evacuate totally the area north of the volcano and the major streams draining the north side, particularly the Toutle River.

Such an evacuation order would have lasted until the bulge had stopped growing and the earthquake activity had died down. This evacuation recommendation would have been made with the idea that it might be weeks before something major happened. Would the public have stood for a vague prediction like this? Would we scientists ourselves have been able to agree on it?

It is worth pointing out here that volcanic prediction has worked very well for the eruptions after May 18. There have been five of these—May 25, June 12, July 22, August 7, and October 16—in the first 6 months, and all have been predicted with sufficient warning to evacuate all scientists, loggers, and other people from the area.

Perhaps the most important lesson to be learned from Mount St. Helens is that volcanoes are dangerous, and they must be taken seriously. Unless memories of government funding agencies are too short, there will be better monitoring of other Cascade volcanoes—Mount Baker, Mount Rainier, Mount Shasta, particularly Mount Hood—than there would have been otherwise. There is a major effort by the USGS and by geologists outside the USGS to learn more about volcanic eruptions, an effort that is due largely to the Mount St. Helens eruptions.

Postscript

In the months following the major eruption of Mount St. Helens and the repeated episodes of dome building, the forces of nature were not gentle with the works of humans.

By January 1982, for example, a series of winter storms had deposited a thick new blanket of snow on the mountain, including a 15-foot- (5-meter-) thick accumulation inside the gaping crater. Then the warm rains moved in off the Pacific Ocean, melting the snow at lower altitudes. The result was a thick slurry of mud that went slithering down into the valleys below. Indeed, by early February the Army Corps of Engineers' expensive sediment-retention dam on the North Fork of the Toutle River lay in ruins, ripped open by the rushing torrent of mud.

And just a few weeks later, new seismic warnings were detected beneath the mountain, indicating that the volcano's winter hibernation was coming to an end. On the night of March 19, a moderate-intensity explosive eruption blasted some rocks off the dome and tossed them southward at the bastionlike headwall of the crater to dislodge an avalanche of snow, rock, and ice. The combined heat from the volcano and friction quickly converted these avalanche materials into a hot flow of mud that came cascading out of the crater's breached north side, where it gouged out a new main channel, rearranging millions of tons of debris and altering the water course, which had been traveled repeatedly for the prior 20 months. This river of mud then rushed past the ruins of the sediment-retention dam and on down into the scoured-out water courses below. The rush of mud quickly raised the water level of the Toutle River by almost 6 feet (2 meters), warmed the river rapidly, and choked aquatic life with silt and debris. Thus nature, in a few hours of frenetic activity, reasserted dominance and warned humans that the future is not at all secure.

Simkin and coworkers report in the Smithsonian Institution's new directory of global volcanoes, *Volcanoes of the World*, that particular eruptions that have attracted media attention have also sparked increased public awareness of volcanoes and led to increased reports of volcanic activity. Fatal eruptions, such as those of Krakatoa in 1883 and Mount Pelée in 1902, resulted in a rash of reports of volcanic activity for nearly a decade thereafter. A similar phenomenon may have developed following the Mount St.

Helens eruption. Since May of 1980, reporters have covered lesser eruptions in Africa, Indonesia, and the Philippines. Most recently, attention has been focused on the March and April 1982 eruptions of remote El Chichon volcano in Mexico, whose ash production significantly dwarfs that of Mount St. Helens.

Noteworthy also is the effect that the Mount St. Helens eruptions are having on volcanic-hazards studies. Once the forgotten step-child of emergency-preparedness agencies, contigency plans in the event of volcanic activity are being revived, reviewed, and modified. Scientific reevaluation of the Cascade volcanoes is also under way. James E. Beget, reporting in the March 12, 1982, issue of *Science*, details a whole string of previously unrecognized volcanic features on Washington State Glacier Peak that have formed since the last major eruption, nearly 12,000 years ago. The most recent volcanic activity occurred only 200 to 300 years ago, indicating a much shorter period of dormancy than previously believed. Although Beget concludes his report with the statement that future volcanic activity at Glacier Peak would probably resemble that of the past several thousand years, he adds that "a sequence of events similar to that which occurred at Mount St. Helens in 1980 . . . is also possible."

Bibliography

Anderson, T., and Flett, J. S., 1903, Report on the eruptions of the Soufriere in St. Vincent, and on a visit to Montagne Pelee in Martinique, part I, *Royal Soc. London Phil. Trans., ser. A* 200, 353–553.

Atwater, T., 1970, Implications of plate tectonics for the Cenozoic tectonic evolution of Western North America, *Geol. Soc. Amer. Bull.*, 81.

Benioff, H., 1954, Orogenesis and deep crustal structure—additional evidence from seismology, *Geol. Soc. Amer. Bull.* 65, 385–400.

Bullard, F. M., 1947, Studies on Paricutin Volcano, Mexico, *Geol. Soc. Amer. Bull.* 58, 433–450.

Bullard, F. M., 1962, *Volcanoes: In History, In Theory, in Eruption*, Austin, University of Texas Press, 441 pp.

Coombs, H. A., and Howard, A. D., 1960, *United States of America*, in *Catalog of Active Volcanoes of the World*, part 9, Naples, International Volcanological Association.

Cotton, C. A., 1952, *Volcanoes as Landscape Forms*, 2nd ed., New York, John Wiley, 416 pp.

Crandell, D. R., 1980, Recent eruptive history of Mt. Hood, Oregon, and potential hazards from future eruptions, *U.S. Geol. Bull.*, 1492.

Crandell, D. R., and Mullineaux, D. R., 1967, Volcanic hazards at Mount Rainier, Washington, *U.S. Geol. Surv. Bull.*, 1238, 26 pp.

Crandell, D. R., and Mullineaux, D. R., 1973, Pine Creek volcanic assemblage at Mount St. Helens, Washington, *U.S. Geol. Surv. Bull.*, 1383-A, 23pp.

Crandell, D. R., and Mullineaux, D. R., 1978, Potential hazards from future eruptions of Mt. St. Helens volcano, Washington, *U.S. Geol. Surv. Bull.*, 1383-C.

Crandell, D. R., Mullineaux, D. R., and Rubin, M., 1975, Mount St. Helens Volcano: recent and future behavior, *Science*, 187, no. 4175, 438–441.

Crandell, D. R., Mullineaux, D. R., and Sigafoos, R. S., 1974, Chaos Crags eruptions and rock-fall avalanches, Lassen Volcanic National Park, California, *Jour. Research, U.S. Geol. Surv.* 2, 49–59.

Crandell, D. R., and Waldron, H. H., 1969, Volcanic hazards in the Cascade range, in Olson, R. A., and Wallace, M. M., *Geologic Hazards and Public Problems*, Office of Emergency Preparedness, pp. 5–18.

Decker, R. W., 1973, State-of-the-art in volcano forecasting: *Bull. Volc.* 37, 372–393.

Decker, R. W., and Decker, B., 1981, *Volcanoes*, San Francisco, Freeman, 244 pp.

Easterbrook, D. J., and Rahm, D. A., 1970, *Landforms of Washington*, Bellingham, WA, Western Washington State College.

Eaton, J. P., and Murata, K. J., 1960, How volcanoes grow, *Science* 132, no. 3432, 925–938.

Evans, M., 1980, The volcano that won't lie down, *New Scientist* 26, 388.

Folsom, M. M., 1970, Volcanic eruptions: the pioneers' attitude on the Pacific Coast from 1800 to 1875: Oregon Dept. of Geology and Mineral Industries, *The Ore Bin* 32, 61–71.

Forsyth, C. E., 1910, Mount St. Helens, *The Mountaineer*, 3, 56–62.

Frank, D., Meier, M. F., and Swanson, D., 1977, Assessment of increased thermal activity at Mt. Baker, Washington, March 1975–March 1976, *U.S. Geol. Surv. Prof. Paper 1022-A.*

Friedman, J. D., and Frank, D., 1980, Infrared surveys, radiant flux, and total heat discharge at Mt. Baker volcano, Washington, between 1970 and 1975, *U.S. Geol. Surv. Prof. Paper 1022-D.*

Greeley, R., and Hyde, J. H., 1972, Lava tubes of the Cave Basalt, Mount St. Helens, Washington, *Geol. Soc. Of Amer. Bull.*, 83.

Gorshkov, G. S. 1959, Gigantic eruption of the volcano Bezymianny: *Bull. Volcanol., Ser. 2* 20, 77–109.

Green, J., and Short, N. M., 1971, *Volcanic Landforms and Surface Features: A Photographic Atlas and Glossary*, New York, Springer-Verlag, 522 pp.

Halliday, W. R., 1963, Features and significance of the Mount St. Helens cave area, *National Parks Magazine*, 37, no. 195, 11–14.

Harris, S. E., 1976, *Fire and Ice, the Cascade Volcanoes*, Seattle, WA, Pacific Search Books, 316 pp.

Hawkins, L. L., 1903, Lava caves of Mount St. Helens, *Mazama* 2, no. 3, 134–135.

Hess, H. H., 1962, History of the ocean basins, *Petrol: Studies Volume in Honor of A. F. Buddington*, Geol. Soc. Amer., pp. 599–620.

Hobbs, P. V., Radke, L. F., Eltgroth, M. W., and Hegg, D. A., 1980, A preliminary report of airborne studies by the Univ. of Wash. of the effluents from the Mt. St. Helens volcanic eruption, Seattle, Univ. of Washington.

Hodgson, J. H., 1964, *Earthquakes and Earth Structure*, Englewood Cliffs, NJ, Prentice-Hall, 166 pp.

Holmes, A., 1965, *Principles of Physical Geology*, 2nd ed., New York, The Ronald Press Company, 1288 pp.

Holmes, K. L., 1955, Mount St. Helens' recent eruptions: *Oregon Historical Quarterly*, vol. 56, pp. 197–210.

Hyde, J. H., 1970, *Geologic Setting of Merrill Lake and Evaluation of Volcanic Hazards in the Kalama River near Mount St. Helens, Washington*, Seattle, 114 pp.

Hyde, J. H., 1973, *Late Quaternary Volcanic Stratigraphy, South Flank of Mount St. Helens, Washington* (Ph.D. thesis), University of Washington, Seattle, 114 pp.

Hyde, J. H., and Crandell, D. R., 1972, Potential volcanic hazards near Mount St. Helens, southwestern Washington (abstract), *Northwest Science Programs and Abstracts.*

Jaggar, T. A., 1904, The initial stages of the spine on Pelee, *Amer. Jour. Sci., 4th Ser.* 17, 34–40.

Jaggar, T. A., 1917, Lava flow from Mauna Loa, 1916, *Amer. Jour. Sci., 4th Ser.* 43, 255–288.

Jaggar, T. A., 1917, Volcanological investigations at Kilauea, *Amer. Jour. Sci., 4th Ser.* 44, 161–220.

Jaggar, T. A., 1947, Origin and development of craters, *Geol. Soc. Amer. Mem.* 21, 508 pp.

Jaggar, T. A., 1949, Steam blast volcanic eruptions, *Hawaiian Volcano Observatory, 4th Special Report*, 137 pp.

Jillson, W. R., 1917, New evidence of a recent volcanic eruption on Mount St. Helens, Washington, *American Journal of Science* 44, no. 259, 59–62.

Judd, J. W., 1888, The eruption of Krakatoa, and subsequent phenomena; on the volcanic phenomena of the eruption, and on the nature and distribution of the ejected materials, *Roy. Soc. London, Krakatoa Comm. Rept.*, pp. 1–56.

Kieffer, S. W., 1981, Blast dynamics at Mount St. Helens on 18 May 1981, *Nature* 291, no. 5816, 568–570.

Korosec, M. A., Rigby, J. G., and Stoffel, K. L., 1980, The 1980 eruption of Mount St. Helens, Washington, Washington State Dept. Nat. Res., Div. Geol. and Earth Res., Info. Circ. 71.

Lamb, H. H., 1970, Volcanic dust in the atmosphere; with a chronology and assessment of its meterological significance, *Roy. Soc. London Phil. Trans.* A266, 425–533.

Landes, H., 1901, The volcanoes of Washington, *Northwest Journal of Education*, 12.

Lawrence, D. B., 1938, Trees on the March, *Mazama* 20, no. 12, 49–54.

Lawrence, D. B., 1939, Continuing research on the flora of Mount St. Helens, *Mazama* 21, no. 12, 49–59.

Lawrence, D. B., 1941, The "Floating Island" lava flow of Mount St. Helens, *Mazama* 23, no. 12, 56–60.

Lawrence, D. B., 1954, Diagrammatic history of the northeast slope of Mount St. Helens, Washington, *Mazama* 36, no. 13, 41–44.

Lawrence, D. B., and Lawrence, E. G., 1958, Bridge of the Gods legend, its origin, history and dating, *Mazama* 40, no. 13, 33–41.

Lawrence, D. B., and Lawrence, E. G., 1959, Radiocarbon dating of some events on Mount Hood and Mount St. Helens, *Mazama* 41, no. 13, 10–18.

Lipman, P. W., and Mullineaux, D. R. (Eds.), 1981, The 1980 eruptions of Mt. St. Helens, Washington, *U.S. Geol. Surv. Prof. Paper 1250.*

MacDonald, G. A., 1943, The 1942 eruption of Mauna Loa, Hawaii, *Amer. Jour. Sci.* 241, 241–256; reprinted in *Smithsonian Ins. Ann. Rept.,* 1943, pp. 199–212.

MacDonald, G. A., 1972, *Volcanoes,* Englewood Cliffs, NJ, Prentice-Hall, 510 pp.

McBirney, A. R., 1963, Factors governing the nature of submarine volcanism, *Bull. Volcan.* 26, 455–469.

McKee, B., 1972, *Cascadia, The Geologic Evolution of the Pacific Northwest,* New York, McGraw-Hill, 394 pp.

Miller, M., 1981, Mount St. Helens eruption—1980, *Am. Alpine Jour.* 23, 99–114.

Moxham, A. R., 1970, Thermal features at volcanoes in the Cascade Range, as observed by aerial infrared surveys, *Bull. Volcan.* 34, 77–106.

Mullineaux, D. R., 1964, Extensive recent pumice lapilli and ash layers from Mount St. Helens volcano, southern Washington (abstract), *Geol. Soc. Amer. Special Paper 76,* p. 285.

Mullineaux, D. R., and Crandell, D. R., 1960, Late recent age of Mount St. Helens volcano, Washington, in *U.S. Geol. Survey Research 1960: Short Papers in the Geol. Sciences,* pp. B307–B308.

Mullineaux, D. R., and Crandell, D. R., 1962, Recent lahars from Mount St. Helens, Washington, *Geol. Soc. Amer. Bull.* 73, 855–870.

Mullineaux, D. R., Hyde, J. H., and Rubin, M., 1972, Preliminary assessment of upper pleistocene and holocene pumiceous tephra from Mount St. Helens, southern Washington (abstract), *Geol. Soc. Amer. Abstracts with Programs* 4, no. 3, 204–205.

Norgren, J. A., Borchardt, G. A., and Harward, M. E., 1970, Mt. St. Helens Y Ash in Northeastern Oregon and South Central Washington (abstract), *Northwest Science* 44, 66.

Ollier, C. D., 1969, *Volcanoes,* Cambridge, MA, MIT Press, 177 pp.

Peck, D. L., Griggs, A. B., Schlicker, H. G., Wells, F. G., and Dole, H. M., 1964, Geology of the central and northern parts of the Western Cascade Range in Oregon, *U.S. Geol. Surv. Prof. Paper 449,* 56 pp.

Peterson, N. V., and Groh, E. A., 1961, Hole-in-the-Ground, central Oregon, *Ore-Bin* 23, 95–100.

Peterson, N. V., 1963, Recent volcanic landforms in central Oregon: Oregon Dept. of Geology and Mineral Industries, *The Ore Bin* 25, no. 3, 33–45.

Phillips, K. N., 1941, Fumaroles of Mount St. Helens and Mount Adams, *Mazama* 23, no. 12, 37–42.

Pryde, P. R., 1968, Mount St. Helens: a possible national monument, *National Parks Magazine* 42, no. 248, 7–10.

Rittman, A., 1962, *Volcanoes and Their Activity,* New York, John Wiley, 305 pp.

Rittman, A., 1973, Explosive volcanic eruptions—a new classification scheme, *Geol. Rundsch.* 62, 431–446.

Rosenfeld, C. L., 1980, Mount St. Helens—an aerial view, *Oregon Geol.* 42, no. 5, 79–85.

Rosenfeld, C. L., 1980, Remote sensing of the Mount St. Helens eruption, May 18, 1980, *Oregon Geol.* 42, no. 6, 103–114.

Rosenfeld, C. L., 1980, Observations on the Mount St. Helens eruption, *Amer. Sci.* 68, no. 5, 494–509.

Rosenfeld, C. L., and Schlicker, H. G., 1976, The significance of increased fumarolic activity at Mount Baker, Washington, *The Ore Bin* 35, no. 2, 23–35.

Russell, I. C., 1897, *Volcanoes of North America,* New York, Macmillan, 346 pp.

Schminky, B., 1954, Records of eruptions of Mount St. Helens: Geol. Soc. Oregon Country, *Geol. News Letter* 20, no. 9, 81–82.

Smith, H. W., Okazaki, R., and Aarsted, J., 1968, Recent volcanic ash in soils of northeastern Washington and southern Idaho, *Northwest Science,* 5.

Taylor, G. A. M., 1958, The 1951 eruption of Mount Lamington, Papua, *Australia Bur. Mineral Resources Geol. Geophys. Bull. 38,* 117 pp.

Tazieff, H., 1962, *Volcanoes,* London Prentice-Hall International.

Unger, J. D., and Mills, K. F., 1973, Earthquakes near Mount St. Helens, Washington, *Geol. Soc. Amer. Bull.* 84, no. 3, 1065–1068.

Verhoogen, J., 1937, *Mount St. Helens, A Recent Cascade Volcano,* California University Publication Geological Science 24, pp. 263–302.

Warrick, R. A., 1975, Volcano hazard in the United States: a research assessment, Inst. Behavioral Sci., Univ. Colorado, 144 pp.

Wexler, H., 1952, Volcanoes and world climate, *Sci. Amer.* 186, no. 4, 74–80.

White, C. M., and McBirney, A. R., 1978, Some quantitative aspects of orogenic volcanism in the Oregon Cascades, *Geol. Soc. Amer. Mem..*

Williams, H., 1935, The Newberry volcano of central Oregon, *Geol. Soc. Amer. Bull.* 46, 253–304.

Williams, H., 1941, *Crater Lake: The Story of Its Origin,* Berkeley, University of Calif. Press, 97 pp.

Williams, H., 1953, *The ancient Volcanoes of Oregon,* 2nd ed., Eugene, OR, Oregon State System of Higher Education, 68 pp.

Williams, H., and McBirney, A. R., 1979, *Volcanology,* San Francisco, Freeman, 397 pp.

Glossary

aa
A Hawaiian term for a rough, highly irregular lava flow in which the molten rock forms into rough, blocky fragments. It seems to flow slowly, by tumbling blocks of rock down its steep front.

andesite
Lava that is intermediate in silica content.

ash
Fragments of volcanic rock less than one-sixth of an inch in diameter, generally finely divided pulverized rock.

basalt
Lava that is relatively poor in silica content, relatively rich in magnesium or iron, and tends to be dark in color.

calderas
Volcanic craters that exceed a mile in diameter. Some are as much as 19 kilometers (12 miles) across and appear to form as a result of collapse, as when an underlying magma chamber has been emptied.

cinder cone
A steep-sided volcanic structure, almost exclusively made up of exploded rock fragments.

composite cone
A volcanic structure composed of alternating layers of exploded rock fragments and lava flows. Such cones tend to be tall and steep sided. Also referred to as stratovolcanoes.

dacite
Lava that is relatively rich in silica content and tends to be thick and viscous.

dome
A volcanic structure built by the extrusion of a highly viscous lava, such as dacite, through a volcanic vent. Lava in a dome tends not to flow, but expands outward by cracking and breaking off in large, blocky chunks.

fumarole
A vent in the ground through which steam and volcanic gases escape. Fumaroles are often marked by deposits of sulfur or other minerals on the surrounding surface.

graben
An elongated depression in the earth's crust, usually lying between two parallel faults.

lava
Liquid or semiliquid molten rock that erupts from a volcano or volcanic vent.

magma
Molten rock that is underground.

magmatic gas
Gases such as carbon dioxide and sulfur dioxide escaping from magma.

mudflows

Vast streams of mud, either hot or cold, that stream down a volcano's sides, reaching speeds of 96 kilometers (60 miles) per hour. They can occur when a "crater lake" drains suddenly, when glaciers melt quickly, or simply when heavy rains mix with loose deposits of ash and dust.

nuées ardentes

"Burning clouds," glowing avalanches of hot ash, rock, and gas, sometimes traveling down a mountainside at 160 kilometers (100 miles) per hour.

obsidian

Volcanic glass, produced by the rapid cooling of lava.

pahoehoe

A Hawaiian term for lava with a smooth, undulating, relatively continuous surface.

phreatic explosion

A steam explosion.

plume

The tall column of ash, dust, and gas thrown into the sky by an erupting volcano.

pumice

Frozen rock froth, often so lightweight it will float on water.

pyroclastic flow

"Fire-broken" fragments of rock that can rush down the flanks of a volcano during an eruption.

rhyolite

A highly acidic type of lava containing 70 to 75 percent silica.

Richter scale

A logarithmic scale denoting the magnitude of an earthquake, that is, the amount of energy released in an earthquake. Earthquakes measured at less than Richter magnitude 3 are usually not felt. Those above magnitude 7.5 or 8 are "great" earthquakes, devastating if centered near populated areas.

shield volcano

A low, broad volcanic structure with gently sloping sides, constructed by repeated flows of relatively liquid lava.

spine

Viscous lava forced up through a volcanic vent to form a tall, tower-like feature. Most such spines erode within a few months.

tectonics

Geophysical activity in the earth's crust, especially the crustal deformation processes such as seafloor spreading and crustal plate collisions.

temblor

An earthquake.

tephra

Pyroclastic or "fire-broken" fragments of rock, classified according to the size of the fragments and their mobility when erupted.

welded tuff

Volcanic ash that remains so hot after coming to rest that the fragments fuse together to form rock.

vent

An opening in the ground through which lava issues. A vent may be long, narrow, and irregular or simply an individual vertical pipe.

volcanic glass

Obsidian, an amorphous material produced by extremely rapid cooling. Obsidian only forms on the ground surface, where contact with cool air prevents crystallization.

Index